It's All About Music
A Memoir

By

John Hsu

Compiled by

Martha Hsu

It's All About Music
A Memoir

To Hella —
with years of fond
memories. Love from

Martha
&
John

To all the inspiring colleagues I had at Cornell University over the years, especially those in the Music Department. In my fifty years there I benefitted enormously from their knowledge, congeniality and good will. I am especially indebted to James Webster for his wisdom and enthusiastic support for all my Haydn endeavors, from the extroverted symphonies to the intimate baryton trios.

Table of Contents

Music, music for awhile
Shall all your cares beguile...

Henry Purcell

Foreword

This memoir is a true collaboration between John and me. John wrote much of the text about five years ago, while he was attending a memoir-writing class. At some point, he created a few shorter accounts of coincidences and humorous events. "My teachers and my cellos" was a separate work. I have incorporated all of these into one narrative, added additional information (with John's suggestions and approval), and selected photographs and other images to insert in the text. Putting it all together was a challenge, given the scope of John's activities. I hope that the table of contents will allow the reader to jump easily to sections of interest.

Friends have often encouraged us to write the story of John's long and unusually interesting life but we have demurred, until now; this is the year we are finally ready to look back. It has been an absorbing experience to elaborate on John's beginnings in China as a boy fascinated with music, soaking up all the instruction he could find, and excelling in whatever he attempted. As he once said, "I learned how to do those things before I knew they were difficult." Making his way as an immigrant in this country, he was dependent on his talent and hard work to succeed. And succeed he did. The second part of the book documents his significant contributions to the beginnings of the period instrument movement, and the wide range of his musical interests and accomplishments.

On a personal note, it is my great good fortune to have been along for the ride, to have been "home-schooled" on how to listen to music, and to have had countless hours of pleasure over the years hearing John practice, rehearse and perform. It's *not* all about music – John is a remarkable person in more ways than one – but music is the dominant and joyful theme that has run through our lives. For that, I am most grateful.

Martha Hsu
Chapel Hill, NC
November, 2015

CHINA

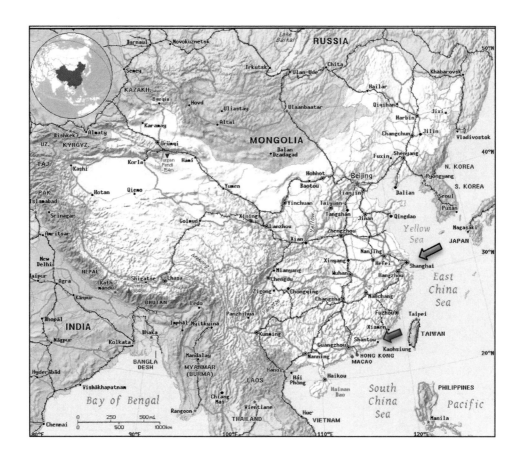

Red arrow points to Shanghai

Blue arrow points to Swatow (Shantou)

Hong Kong is west of Swatow

My Father's Family

Father's father

Father's mother

One day early in 1898, in the southern Chinese seaport of Swatow (now called Shantou), a weary young couple put their children to bed in their modest living quarters after a day of exhausting labor. They were once again mulling over what steps they should take and what changes they should make in order to improve the quality of their lives and give their children a more promising future. They had been asking themselves this grave question for the last few months, ever since they knew that another infant was on its way. They already had two sons and a daughter, and they were determined to give them all the best possible education.

The father was a retail butcher with a portable meat stall that enabled him to ply his business at the pier and in some rich residential areas where the customers had the means to buy the best cuts. The couple realized that such a business had its limitations, and they needed to find a way to improve their lot for their children's sake. After months of agonizing indecision and fervent prayers, that night, with their new Christian faith and their belief that God would guide them to a brighter future, they made the decision to go into the linen and silk embroidery business. The mother had learned to do embroidery from the Christian missionaries. This new skill, that she had mastered quickly and with relative ease, not only noticeably augmented their income, but also gave her a wonderful feeling of artistic satisfaction never known to her before. In time, a steady stream of orders for her products from exporters and local retail stores necessitated her hiring other skillful embroiderers to meet the demand.

The new infant born in March of that year was a boy, who in time became my father. Two more siblings followed, a brother and a sister. The family business prospered steadily while they grew up. Except for the oldest brother, who was needed to help the parents with their business and who managed the enterprise after his father's death, all the children received the best possible education, attending colleges and universities in Shanghai.

Having received many blessings through the teachings of Christianity, it was not surprising that the parents thought it fitting that one of their sons would devote his life to the service of the Christian church. My father went to the U.S. for his master's degree from Princeton and his Ph.D. from the University of Hartford in Connecticut. (Perhaps the missionaries were helpful in suggesting overseas possibilities for his graduate education.) During his summers in the U.S. in the 1920s, he was able to help support himself by selling his family's linen and silk embroideries in a resort hotel in Gloucester, Massachusetts. The embroidery business turned out to be a considerable family asset— one that benefitted me as well when I came to this country in 1949.

My Mother's family

Mother's parents

On March 28, 1906, in the city of Heifong, Kwangtung province, a young government official in the Ministry of Finance and his family were celebrating the birth of their second child. Although it was a daughter, they were genuinely happy, for they already had a son. Moreover, they had planned to have a large family, so there would be plenty of time to arrive at a desirable balance. The celebration was not a lavish one, for in spite of his intellectual brilliance and promising future, having passed the government's test for officials and holding an important government position, the father was not a man of means. But the presence of love and contentment in this home was palpable to all who entered it.

It began from the day of their wedding. Like most marriages of the time, theirs was arranged by their parents, and the bride and groom did not meet until their wedding day. According to the bride, she was so worried about the appearance of her future husband that, the first chance she had, she pulled aside the curtain of her sedan chair to have a peek at him before the wedding ceremony. She was so happy that Fate had brought her such a handsome man that she literally fell in love with him at first sight. With the passage of time together, she came to appreciate all his other virtues as well. She was a woman who had the capacity to love and enjoy her family and all the beautiful things in life. She was also optimistic and wise. To this day, when I think of her I hear her hearty laughter and remember her answer to the question of how one could live with an arranged marriage. Her answer was: "How does one boil water? Start cold."

Together they had ten children; four sons and four daughters survived into adulthood. Of these, the oldest daughter in time became my mother. The first two sons studied economics in Paris and returned home to become businessmen. Of the five other siblings, two sons and two daughters became professional musicians.

Number 4, a son, Ma Sicong, was a famous violinist/composer and the first President of the Central Conservatory of Music in Beijing. During the Cultural Revolution he was humiliated and tortured before somehow managing to escape by boat to Hong Kong. Eventually he settled in Philadelphia.

Number 8 was a daughter, Ma Si-Ju, who became a cellist, teaching at the Beijing conservatory. She and her husband, an architect who had studied with I.M. Pei, were in Beijing in 1989 during the Tiananmen uprising. She insisted on going to see what was happening and by chance was caught on camera as NBC News filmed the crowd. Also by chance, her daughter, who was living in Florida with her family at the time, happened to see her mother on the news and was able to snap the TV screen with a handy Polaroid camera as her mother was shown.

On August 11, 2008, NBC aired a show called "Changes in China Over the Last 30 Years." It featured Brian Williams talking with Tom Brokaw about Brokaw's many trips to China. One of his assistants was a young woman named Titi Yu– the daughter of the couple in Florida and the granddaughter of the cellist in Beijing! She showed Brokaw the 1989 snapshot of her mother on TV and Brokaw liked the idea of interviewing Titi's grandmother for the show. So my aunt was shown on the evening news, in her apartment and walking down the street with Titi and Tom Brokaw, reminiscing about the events of 1989.

Number 9, Ma Si-Hon, was a well-known violinist in the U.S. He played with the Cleveland Orchestra for a time, then taught for many years at Kent State University. He and his pianist wife, Tung Kwong-Kwong, toured as a duo, giving many concerts here and in China. Kwong-Kwong had a sister who settled in Ithaca, New York, with her husband, who taught Mechanical and Aerospace Engineering at Cornell University for many years and thus was a colleague of mine there.

Number 10, a daughter, played flute in the Symphony Orchestra in Beijing.

One of the sons who had gone to Paris to study economics met and married a French woman, who returned home with him. Aunt Yvonne was a fun-loving woman who introduced me to French regional food, including mutton. During the Cultural Revolution, my uncle was ridiculed because of his French wife, and after he died she had to leave China.

My Parents

Benjamin and Lucy Ma Zi

My parents met in Shanghai during the summer of 1927, when my father returned home for a visit after earning his master's degree from Princeton University. It was a well-deserved holiday for him before returning to the U.S. to pursue a Ph.D. the following academic year. This was a long-awaited homecoming trip to which he had looked forward with great anticipation, eager to see his family and the fiancée whom he had left behind. Imagine the shock, sadness, and heartbreak when upon arrival he was confronted with the news that his intended had jilted him in his absence! It was at this seemingly inauspicious moment that my parents met. They must have fallen for each other right away. He was an attractive, energetic and decisive fellow, and she a beautiful, courageous, and devoted woman. By the end of the summer of wooing, they agreed that she should join him in the U.S. where they would wed. It was with such an impassioned, bold, and trusting commitment that they began to build their life together.

My mother was a brave woman. She traveled alone out of China for the first time, across the Pacific and across the U.S. to meet her intended, not speaking the English language very well and not knowing what her life would be like in a foreign country. But she had a tranquil temperament. My father years later told the story of meeting the train when she was due to arrive. Pacing the platform, he anxiously watched everyone emerge from the train before she finally sauntered off last – a good illustration of the difference in their personalities!

My mother attended the Northfield College for Women in Massachusetts the following academic year. My parents were married in Hartford, CT, in 1929, and their first daughter, Nancy, was born in June of 1930, the month when my father received his Ph.D. from the University of Hartford. What an abundance of joy they had that year! And exciting new responsibilities awaited them in China.

That summer, they returned to our hometown, Swatow, where my father had accepted a dual appointment as director of the Bailey Theological Seminary and pastor of the Presbyterian Church, beginning in the fall. It was shortly after that trip that I sneaked into their lives. I emerged in Swatow prematurely on April 21, 1931.

Swatow (Shantou)

Swatow is located fewer than 200 miles east along the coast from Hong Kong. Its latitude is comparable to that of Havana, Cuba; it has a humid, subtropical climate. In 1936, Swatow was the second biggest port in South China, second only to Canton. Its chief export to the U.S. at that time was embroidery (some of it my grandmother's work), for which Swatow was famous.

In my memory, Swatow was a paradise of tropical pleasures, not least of which was wonderful fruit. After my brother Tom joined the family in 1933, my parents hired a nanny to help. One pre-breakfast ritual I particularly liked, and which happened quite frequently, was an

Nanny

excursion to the garden with the nanny to pick a fig or two from the fig tree. She would ask me choose a fig, then she would cut the chosen one with scissors on a stick and the fig would fall into the waiting basket. Then we would stop at the hen house where I could pick out a warm egg before going inside and having some wonderful fresh congee (a soupy rice similar to hot cereal in consistency). Years later, when Martha and I visited Hong Kong in 1971, my nanny made a long bus ride to see us, bringing, with great difficulty, her freshly made turnip cake -- because she remembered how much I had loved it as a child. She died soon thereafter.

Since my father was the Director of the Bailey Theological Seminary, we had a house at one end of the seminary compound. It had a beautiful garden between the rear of the house and the gate that led to the main street beyond the seminary walls. Near the end of the garden, near the gate and the wall, were two swings for Nancy and me.

The rest of the garden was full of flowers. The seminary's gardener worked in this garden and kept it beautiful. I still recall overhearing a visitor saying to my father after admiring the garden, "Reverend, you do not have to go to paradise. This is paradise!"

Nancy, John, Tom, and our mother

My Early Years in Music

I have often been asked when I began studying music and how I decided to become a professional musician. With genes from my mother's side and the helpful influence of her siblings, I think that embarking on the path of music was very much pre-ordained.

I cannot be certain whether I began piano lessons at age three or four. They most likely came about because my sister, Nancy, was taking lessons and clearly enjoying them. My lessons lasted between one and two years, ending in 1936 when our family left Swatow due to the increasing threat of the impending Sino-Japanese war.

Of those early lessons, I do not remember anything relating to their musical content. I was probably a good pupil, for I have only happy memories of playing the instrument -- no struggles, no obstacles to overcome, no severe criticism. My teacher, Miss Yang, must have given me a good foundation, for when I continued piano lessons in Shanghai after a hiatus of two years I was able to resume my progress and recapture my enthusiasm.

In retrospect, I now realize that learning to play the piano was not the only enjoyable experience I had at Miss Yang's. In the small front-yard of her modest home, she often had a few cute little white chicks. After almost eight decades, I can still feel the wonderfully soft and warm sensation of holding one of them snuggled in my hands. This happened often enough that it somehow became a part of the music-lesson experience that I enjoyed.

I have no recollection of what Miss Yang looked like. She was probably a young woman of average stature. But I do remember her as a gentle person of great warmth, and I looked forward each week to sitting on the piano bench with her. She was the first person who transmitted to me the joy of music making and consequently the one who planted the seed that, with subsequent nourishment and cultivation, led to the growth of a musician.

Miss Yang's home was not the only place where I encountered music. The other venue was the church. My father was at the time pastor of a quite splendid church in Swatow, where on Sundays and at weddings I heard hymns and other sacred music sung by the choir and the congregation. I was too young to judge the sophistication of the music or the standard of the performance, but I was always moved by the sound of group singing and the fervor with which the music was sung. My father had a rich baritone voice and could be heard leading the congregation in singing the hymns. There in the ambience of the church I got acquainted with the feeling of solemnity through music.

Weddings were the most exciting events in the church. They were occasions when music called forth not only solemnity, but also great happiness. For me, it was also a ceremony in which I got to play an important part. From the time that I was old enough to do so, I was frequently the ring boy in weddings that were large enough to call for one. I loved getting dressed up in my formal black-and-white silk outfit, carrying a silk cushion with the wedding ring on it, and marching down the aisle in time with the music.

I played this role often enough that I knew the complete marriage ritual by heart. One day my nanny reported to my parents that I had officiated a wedding ceremony between two neighborhood children who were willing to allow me to marry them. Although amused, my father forbade me from doing it again, and I never did. But my fascination with weddings continued. It was from them that I learned the important truth that one weeps from happiness as well as sadness, and that music can arouse both emotions. To this day I find it difficult to stop myself from shedding a tear at weddings.

Two Years in Hong Kong

The war with Japan started in July of 1937 and continued for eight years. Our family decided to evacuate from Swatow, which was a vulnerable seaport. We went first to Hong Kong, where relatives could house us temporarily. Whether intended or not, we ended up spending about two years there as refugees, moving from one cramped lodging to another.

Needless to say, the transition to Hong Kong was puzzling and abrupt for a child. It was a total surprise when our family arrived at the home of my father's oldest brother to find that, because of the twelve cousins already living there, our family was to be ensconced temporarily in the garage. I disliked Hong Kong immediately. Compared with Swatow, it was crowded, noisy and messy. Even though I was only five or six years old and was told that our situation was temporary, I felt ashamed when emerging from the garage each day.

While in Hong Kong I attended St. Mary's Primary School along with Nancy. I do not remember anything about this school except that I had to wear a uniform – a blue and white quasi-sailor style school uniform: the same top with skirts for girls and shorts for boys. I thought the uniform was silly in appearance and unbecoming for boys to wear, so I shed it as soon as possible each day.

It was in Hong Kong that, perhaps for self-defense, I developed the ability to forget events, experiences, and feelings that I found too upsetting and hurtful. Consequently, I retain no clear picture or sense of continuity of our stay there. We moved several times but I do not remember any addresses. Needless to say, there was no piano to be had, and hence no music. It is as though my life went from Swatow in 1936 to Shanghai in 1938 or 1939.

Schools in Shanghai

After two years in Hong Kong, we relocated to Shanghai. Moving from place to place exposed me to different dialects and made it necessary for me to learn the dialects taught and spoken in the schools at each place. The Swatow dialect was spoken only in Swatow; Cantonese was the local language in Hong Kong; the Shanghai dialect was different from both. In Shanghai my school also required fluency in Mandarin. Consequently I had to repeat fourth grade.

Shanghai was a large, cosmopolitan city of millions in population even then, with all kinds of schools available. For ease in transportation during the first year or two, Nancy, Tom, and I attended a small grade school only two blocks from our house. It was a bi-lingual grade school called Peter Pan School, owned and run by its British principal, Mrs. Ann Taylor and a few teachers, both Chinese- and English-speaking. We all began learning Shanghai dialect, Mandarin, and English when studying there.

It was in Mrs. Taylor's English class that I learned my first English poem, a simple quatrain entitled "Self-control."

> Self-control is a very good thing
> Better than a diamond ring
> For a diamond ring can be lost far away
> But self-control is with you to stay.

Mrs. Taylor must have been pleased with my English pronunciation, because I was called upon to recite this poem at least once at some kind of school convocation.

It was at the next school that I really understood and appreciated the seriousness of learning and the variety of subjects that one could study. Its Chinese name was simply "The World." It had a reputation for high educational standards and student achievement. The attending students

were frequently reminded that, if they did not do well, there were many others waiting to take their places. (There were no free public schools in those days so all the students' families paid tuition.)

It was in this school that I was exposed to Japanese, the occupiers' language, taught during the war. The teacher, who was a Korean man imported from his own Japanese-occupied country, didn't want to teach Japanese and the students didn't want to learn it, so the class consisted of the students answering every question with the Japanese phrase that meant, "I don't understand." This handy phrase could have been put to good use many years later, in front of Carnegie Hall in New York, when I was asked a question in Japanese by a Japanese tourist. Only "could have been," because, put on the spot, I could not remember the answer until the moment had passed!

Other than walking, the mode of transportation to school was predominantly the bicycle. (A few very rich kids were delivered to school by chauffeured limousines.) My siblings and I went to school on two bikes. My younger sister Bella, born in 1936, rode on the back seat of Nancy's bike, and Tom rode behind me on mine.

This arrangement ceased when Nancy started attending high school at a Catholic convent school known for its high scholastic standards, and I chose to go to the Associated High School of the University of Shanghai (Hujiang University), which was located downtown, more than thirty minutes ride on the bike. I went there for only a year and a half, after which I transferred to the Shanghai American School for tenth grade. By then I was eager to improve my English ability in preparation for studies in the U.S.

Young family in Shanghai

Early Musical Training in Shanghai

It was a stroke of good fortune that found our family ensconced in a large house in Shanghai that belonged to my aunt (my father's younger sister) and her husband. Since he was a government official, they had to live in Chungking at the time, and therefore welcomed our family as house sitters during their absence.

We were greeted in Shanghai by Cousin Helen, the daughter of my father's older sister, who was living in the house while attending college there. Fortunately for me, she was a lovely person and a fine pianist. She took an interest in my piano playing and offered me lessons. She was a most encouraging teacher, and gradually introduced me to the great composers: Bach, Haydn, Mozart, and Beethoven, among others. Since their works were relatively recent musical discoveries for her, she was spontaneously enthusiastic and impassioned in imparting her love and admiration for the music. She also instilled in me a serious attitude towards music, and made me aware of the need eventually to study music theory. I had almost four years of fruitful lessons with her until her graduation from college and departure from Shanghai.

In this big house, where we lived until the end of World War II, there was a large living room/ballroom and a piano. In this spacious room the choir of my father's church held its rehearsals during the war years. Here is where I first got acquainted with well-sung sacred choral music. The members of the choir were mostly college students, and the choir director was Professor Chou Mei-Pa, a fine Belgian-trained Chinese musician. The keyboard accompanist was a short, quiet Viennese musician by the name of Wolff (either I never knew his first name or have forgotten it).

Mr. Wolff seemed to be able to do anything on demand. Not only could he sight-read any piece of music put in front of him, but he could also transpose the music to any key (pitch level) that the choir director wished. On festive occasions, when the director wanted an orchestral accompaniment for works for which orchestral parts were unavailable,

Mr. Wolff was able to write out all the parts for all the players. To an eleven-year old, his musical prowess was like magic.

It was frustrating that I could not really converse with him and get to know him better because he knew no Chinese, I knew no German, and our English was very limited. Nonetheless, I gradually insinuated myself into his proximity by offering to be his page-turner when he needed one, and I somehow was able to convey to him my desire to learn something about music theory from him. I began to attend these weekly Thursday afternoon choir rehearsals regularly, and whenever he was free afterwards he would give me a short lesson. In time, he taught me the rudiments of four-part harmony and the concept of good part writing, mostly by means of written musical examples. If I wrote a good example, he would say, "*Gut.*" If it had problems, he would say, "*Schlecht.*" From this tutoring and the simplified chords that he played when accompanying the choir, I got my first inkling of good harmony.

Occasionally, my parents would invite Mr. Wolff to stay for dinner after the lessons. From his appearance and demeanor we were aware that he was often hungry, and the sharing of those meals somehow brought us closer despite the lack of a common language for any substantive conversation. By then, he and I shared not only our love of music but also our experience of suffering from hunger. Mr. Wolff died shortly before the end of the war.

The War Years in Shanghai

Our family was more fortunate than many, but the war years were difficult nonetheless. Food was rationed and, more often than not, no matter what the coupon said, lima beans appeared. To this day I cannot eat lima beans with pleasure. Rice was routinely laced with small pebbles and it was my job and that of my siblings to sort out the rice from the pebbles. There was no sugar to be had. (Hence my sweet tooth?) Worst of all was the cold. Shanghai's winters were bitterly cold, with overnight temperatures sometimes far below freezing, and our house had no central heating. Some people got TB from malnutrition and cold; I had asthma. The most difficult memory I have from the war is of seeing on the street the bodies of people who had frozen to death the previous night.

In spite of the ravages of the war years, we, the children, were richly blessed with neighborhood friendships. We were living in the residential part of the French Concession. It so happened that we lived in one of three adjacent homes that had four children in each family, seven boys in all. They were the Hou family, the Fan family, and ours. We were close enough in age so that we could all play as equals. We played rambunctious games like cops and robbers, cerebral games like bridge and chess, and sports like soccer and ping pong. Since the Hous had the largest house and lawn, we mostly played there after school. This became a routine for four or five years, all through the war. I cannot recall any incidents that caused hard feelings or ill will. It was wonderful that seven boys could enjoy each other's company and play so harmoniously for such an extended period of time! Our sisters also became friends through these years.

But once we began to attend different high schools and to pursue our individual pre-professional interests, it became difficult to maintain the cohesiveness of our youthful friendship. By the end of the war, the demands of my musical pursuits on my time outside school were so great that I had to give up being a dependable part of the group. This coincided with my brother Tom's decision to attend high school at a boarding school in Soochow, which removed him from the neighborhood

20

altogether. During our college years we all lost touch with our former neighbors.

Then, over twenty years later, a miraculous incident occurred. Sometime in the middle 1970's, I went to lecture and play at the University of Southern California in Los Angeles. One evening, while dining in a Chinese restaurant, a charming and well-dressed woman about my age tapped me on the shoulder and said "Hello, John." I must have looked puzzled as I said, truthfully, that I did not recognize her. She said, "Don't you remember your old neighbor from Shanghai? I am Laura Fan, sister of Bob and Benny." With that declaration of identity, of course I saw immediately the young Laura in front of me, followed by a flood of accumulated memories of thirty years before.

Naturally I asked her whether she knew anything about the Hou family. The incredible answer was that three of the four Hou siblings were at that very moment outside in the parking lot waiting for her, for they had just finished having dinner together. She went and fetched them and we had an unexpected reunion right then and there. When we finally finished bringing ourselves up-to-date, May Hou, the oldest daughter of the family and my sister Nancy's best friend, ended with a message for Nancy. "Tell Nancy and her husband Paul to consider settling in Glendale, California, when they return to this country from Hong Kong, so we can be neighbors again." And that was just what happened: they became neighbors again.

Jewish Refugees in Shanghai

In Europe, during the 1930's, the Jews were desperate to escape, especially after *Kristallnacht* in 1938, but most had few options. There was only one place in the world where they could go without a visa or any other paperwork: Shanghai. There were two main ways to get there -- by ship via Italy (until June 1940 when Italy entered the war) and by land across Russia and through Siberia. Despite multiple uncertainties and hardships, over 17,000 refugees from central Europe arrived in Shanghai between 1938 and 1941. Some estimates of the total number of European Jewish refugees in Shanghai during the war are as high as 30,000.

At the time, Shanghai was a city of over four million Chinese and nearly 100,000 foreigners. The Japanese had occupied the city since 1937. Their attitude toward the Jews was complex but generally neutral. It wasn't until February of 1943 that the occupiers acceded to pressure from the Nazis and established a ghetto in Hongkew (a section of the Shanghai International Settlement) where all so-called stateless refugees were required to live. Less than one square mile in area, Hongkew became the new home for the refugees who joined the 100,000 Chinese who already lived there.

Conditions were cramped and difficult. Exits were guarded but it was occasionally possible to get a pass to leave, and residents from outside could visit. Various international aid agencies were crucial in supplying food and other assistance. In July of 1945, American bombers attacked a Japanese radio station located in Hongkew, killing 40 Jewish refugees and hundreds of Chinese. The war ended in China shortly thereafter with the bombing of Hiroshima and Nagasaki in August.

Musical Training in Shanghai after the War

After the end of the war, Shanghai was transformed practically overnight from a dark and moribund city occupied by the Japanese army to a bright, cheerful, victorious metropolis, in spite of constant reminders of the devastation of the war. For musicians and music lovers in the city, the dissolution of the Hongkew ghetto was perhaps the most influential source of inspiration. For the German- and Austrian-Jewish musicians who lived there, liberation meant that they could now travel freely throughout the city to play and teach music. The local music students who hungered for instruction and inspiration during the war years were impatient to seek the best of what this extraordinary group of European musicians had to offer.

I had worked diligently on the piano during the war years, taught by Cousin Helen, whose fine teaching made me aware of the importance of music theory. Luckily, after an interview that included playing the piano, I was accepted as a private student of the most sought-after music theory teacher in the city.

Wolfgang Fraenkel[1] (1897-1983), composer, theorist, performer, and conductor, was not only a superb and versatile musician, but also a very learned man, trained in law as well as music. He had been a judge at the Court of Appeals in Berlin from 1923 until April of 1933, when Hitler removed all Jews from public office. Thereafter, he worked as a freelance musician in Berlin until his departure for Shanghai in 1939, after his release from the Sachsenhausen concentration camp, where he had briefly been detained.

His presence, until his emigration to the U.S. in late 1947, was to have a lasting and profound influence on the development of western music in

---

[1] "Cultural Accommodation and Exchange in the Refugee Experience: A German-Jewish Musician in Shanghai"
Christian Utz
Ethnomusicology Forum
Vol. 13, No. 1, January 2004, pp. 119-151

Shanghai, especially for serious music students. He taught not only all the advanced students at the music conservatory, but he also took on a number of private students during weekends. I was most fortunate to have been one of his private students for two whole years. From these intensive private lessons I learned advanced harmony, counterpoint, form and analysis, and orchestration. It was this study of orchestration and major orchestral works that gave me the idea of learning the cello, not so much with the intention of becoming a professional cellist as to be a more versatile and knowledgeable musician. However, this attitude changed quickly, due mainly to the inspiration of my first cello teacher. I soon became enamored with the instrument and decided to become a cellist.

Johann Kraus, my first cello teacher, was the erstwhile first cellist of the Berlin State Opera. Like Mr. Fraenkel, he also had fled Nazi Germany in the late 1930's and ended up in Shanghai. In spite of the privation of the war years there, he managed to maintain the high standard of his playing to the extent that, when he immigrated to the U.S. in late 1947, in his sixties, he was invited to join the San Francisco Symphony Orchestra, and with this distinguished group added ten more years to his musical career. An especially touching and nostalgic event in San Francisco was the reunion with Bruno Walter, his old friend from Berlin days. Best of all, after he settled in San Francisco, his wife was able to join him there to continue their married life after a separation of some 15 years!

Johann Kraus and Bruno Walter

To this day, I remember my first meeting with Mr. Kraus. I fully realized that back in his Berlin days he would not have deigned to consider teaching someone like me, someone who wanted to study the cello with him but was a beginner who could not play anything on the cello. So I played the piano instead. As I was eager to show him that at least I was not a musical beginner, I played for him the difficult Liszt Etude in D-flat Major, with lots of fast notes and hand-crossings. When I finished playing, he nodded his head and said something like, "Not bad, but one has to keep in mind that a cellist usually plays but one note at a time, and if that note is not just right and meaningful, one has nothing to say musically." He was a fine cellist and disciplinarian, from whom I learned not only how to play, but also how to listen discriminatingly.

Before Mr. Kraus left Shanghai, he recommended that I continue cello lessons with Walter Joachim (1912-2001), a brilliant, younger German Jewish cellist from Dusseldorf and Cologne. During 1940-51 he served as head of the cello department at the Shanghai Conservatory of Music and was principal cellist of the Shanghai Symphony Orchestra. When he first arrived in Shanghai he worked in a menial job during the day and played cello in a café and dancehall at night. I remember hearing him and his brother Otto playing at the "Silk Hat." On one occasion I enjoyed a coffee while he had a whiskey at a café in the district called "Little Vienna," which was populated by European style cafés, shops, and nightclubs operated by Viennese refugees.

I studied with him until I left Shanghai in early 1949. From him I learned what real cello virtuosity and romanticism meant. His playing was so distinctive and moving that, years later, I could recognize it when I happened to hear his performance on a radio broadcast. From that broadcast I learned that he had become principal cellist of the Montreal Symphony Orchestra. I surprised him with a visit when I was next at McGill University, where he was the cello professor from 1952 until his retirement.

During my last year in Shanghai, after Mr. Fraenkel's departure, I continued the study of music theory with Julius Schloss (1902-1973), his successor at the Shanghai Conservatory of Music, who had been a student of Alban Berg (one of the most influential composers of the 20th century) in Vienna. Although I was then too young fully to understand and appreciate his teaching, his introduction to me of Arnold Schoenberg's new twelve-tone technique of composition was crucial in helping me learn to play Schoenberg's Third String Quartet at the Berkshire Music Center, Tanglewood, in the summer of 1950.

The end of the war also brought to a close the imprisonment of American and British citizens in Japanese-controlled internment camps in Shanghai. Thus it was possible again to study with the expert musicians among them. From pre-war days, Robert Vivian Dent was considered the leading organist in Shanghai. As organist and choirmaster of the American Community Church of Shanghai, he presided over the best and largest organ and occupied the most prestigious church position in the city. He was also a fine pianist. Although he taught only a limited number of students, he consented to take me as a piano student early in 1946. He was such a knowledgeable and versatile musician that my lessons with him gradually expanded to include discussions of choral music, keyboard harmony and improvisation.

In the spring of 1948, the congregation of the Church had grown so large that an earlier Sunday morning service was added and a director for the new Chancel Choir was needed. Thanks to Mr. Dent's recommendation, I was offered the position. The experience that I gained during that year was to serve me well much later in my professional life. With this choir, we performed "The Holy Child," a Christmas Cantata by the respected American composer Horatio Parker (Dean of the School of Music at Yale University from 1904 to 1919) on Christmas Day in 1948.

Christmas

"THE HOLY CHILD"

A Christmas Cantata
by
Horatio W. Parker
sung by
THE CHANCEL CHOIR
directed by
JOHN HSU
Miss MARGARET YUAN, ORGANIST

with the CHAPEL SINGERS as the
CAROLLERS
•
Wendell Flory
Narrator
•
J. Hood Snavely,
Pastor
•
6:00 p.m. Christmas Day
Saturday, December 25, 1948
THE
COMMUNITY CHURCH OF SHANGHAI

Thus it was that during my high school years (1946-49) I undertook a demanding regimen of musical training that included private lessons in cello, piano and music theory from the best possible teachers anywhere. Under normal circumstances these musicians would not have taken a student as young and untrained as I was. But circumstances were far from normal, and I benefitted from the tragic events of the war years.

27

The Shanghai American School

By 1947, my parents had acceded to my desire to prepare myself for a career in music, and also agreed that the best place to go for my further studies was the U.S. To prepare myself for going to America and to improve my English, I decided to attend the Shanghai American School for my last two years of high school.

The Shanghai American School first opened its doors in 1912. At first the students came from missionary families, but soon children came from business, consular, and military service backgrounds as well. Having closed for a time during the Second World War while the Japanese occupied the city, it reopened in 1946. Despite the struggle going on in Shanghai, and indeed in all of China, between the Nationalists and the Communists, American and European businesses started up in Shanghai during the post war years, supplying children for S.A.S. However, by 1948, inflation was unchecked and the Communists were winning the civil war, so Westerners began to leave Shanghai and other areas of China. The Communists took over Shanghai in May of 1949 and the school closed.

The students at S.A.S during 1946-49 shared a special bond that has lasted into the 21st century. Reunions are enthusiastically attended and the newsletter has a broad readership. My most lasting contribution to the school was a musical one. The students in 1947-48 decided that S.A.S. needed an official alma mater and held a contest to select one. All the other students suggested existing melodies, but I wrote an original song. Another classmate wrote the words, we entered the competition, and we won. With its inclusion in the history of the school, Fair is the Name: the Story of the Shanghai American School, 1912-1950, by Phoebe White Wentworth and Angie Mills (Los Angeles, Shanghai American School Association, 1997), I became a published composer!

S.A.S. School Song

Music by John Hsu
Words by Ted Stannard

Preparing for Study Abroad

In the late 1940s, before there were tape recordings, a music student applying to colleges and music schools was required to appear in person to perform before a jury or a person of authority, especially when applying for financial aid. Thus I found myself in a catch-22 situation -- I was unable to go to the U.S. for auditions because of the lack of a visa, but I was unable to obtain a visa unless I received admission and sufficient scholarship aid from a school. So for a time, my hope of studying abroad appeared stymied.

In life, as in a play or a novel, such a moment is often resolved by the appearance of a *deus ex machina*. In this case, it came in an offer of admission and a tuition scholarship from Carroll College in Waukesha, Wisconsin. This manna from heaven, seemingly miraculous, was actually the result of an uncle's persistent and thoughtful research on potential sources of financial aid for an undergraduate music student like me. This uncle (the father of cousin Helen, who taught me piano during the four years she lived with our family while attending university in Shanghai) was a highly respected headmaster of a prep school in Swatow, our hometown, and fortuitously was then spending a sabbatical year in the U.S. How he became familiar with Carroll College I do not know, but he encouraged me to apply to this institution for two reasons: 1) the presence on its music faculty of a fine cellist, Josef Schroetter, and 2) its affiliation with the Presbyterian Church, which he thought would probably make the college more inclined to help the son of a Presbyterian pastor, which I was. Subsequent events proved him right. Carroll College forewent an audition and accepted me based solely upon the letters of recommendation from my European music teachers in Shanghai. I never knew what they wrote on my behalf, but their evaluation and opinion succeeded in securing for me a tuition-free scholarship to attend Carroll College for the academic year 1949-50, with the possibility of earning enough for my room and board by doing janitorial work in the college library.

This wonderful news reached me and my family amidst the deteriorating situation in Shanghai, as a result of the armed struggles between the

Communist Party and the Nationalist Party. Once again, my parents decided that it would be more secure to evacuate to Hong Kong, while making arrangements for my travel abroad. There were so many families of students at the Shanghai American School who planned to leave Shanghai before the end of the academic year that the School allowed us to complete our last semester of high school elsewhere and be granted an S.A.S. diploma. Consequently, I completed my high school education at the American School in Hong Kong.

In August of 1949, after a long and frustrating year of uncertainties and delays in the process of securing the necessary travel documents for my trip to study in the U.S., I finally got my passport from the Chinese government and my visa from the U.S. government. By then it was too late for me to book passage on any ocean liner that would have brought me to the U.S. in time for the new academic year. In desperation, my parents managed to scrape together enough money to pay for an airline ticket for me to cross the Pacific. Boarding the airplane alone for the long flight I realized that I had no idea when I would see my parents again or what the future had in store for me, but I was full of impatience and eager to get on with my education.

My Airline Flight to America (Martinis)

In the pre-jet age there were no direct flights from Hong Kong to the U.S., so this long 40-hour flight was divided into two parts. The first leg of the trip, taking most of a day, was from Hong Kong to Yokohama on a BOAC seaplane. The passengers were then bused to Tokyo and put up overnight at the famous Ambassador Hotel. The second part of the flight took over 33 hours: Tokyo to Anchorage, with a stop in the Aleutian Islands for re-fueling and change of crew, then on to Seattle. This long flight was on a huge Northwest Airlines plane called a Stratocruiser.

The Stratocruiser was the commercial airline version of the four-engine Boeing B-29 Superfortress bomber, combined with a bulbous fuselage. The sleeper part of this large-capacity long-distance double-decker plane in which I was traveling was equipped with 28 sleeping berths and five seats. On the lower deck was also a beverage lounge/game room. Soon after the takeoff, the stewards and stewardesses began serving complimentary drinks and food, interspersed between scheduled meals. This went on non-stop until our landing in Anchorage.

Since the Stratocruiser had just begun service to Hong Kong that year, such an extended flight was a new experience for all the passengers on board, so everyone was too keyed up to think of sleeping for quite a while. I was one of four passengers who chose to play bridge in the lounge after the first dinner. We must have played through most of the night. It was during this long bridge game that I had my first three Martinis.

It so happened that when we sat down to play bridge, the lounge steward asked us what we would like to drink. One of the players ordered a Martini and the others had the same. I went along, having no idea what else to order. When the steward came back a while later for orders, my bridge partners asked for refills. So when the steward returned for the third time, I cheerfully ordered another round of refills. That was how I was initiated into hard liquor. After that, the sleeping berth was absolute bliss.

I was met at the Seattle airport by a kind, distant relative and her husband, neither of whom I had met before. I called her "Aunt Louise" because she belonged to my parents' generation. She was the sister of the sister-in-law of one of my father's sisters-in-law. Such was the breadth

 of our family network available to my parents when seeking assistance for their son. I was very happy to meet her family and stay overnight at their home. Before I left for San Francisco the following day, Aunt Louise took my picture, then generously sent me off with a paper bag lunch of fried chicken drumsticks for the train ride. They were so delicious that I still remember them with appreciation and gratitude.

The Tablecloth

Given my family's close association with Swatow embroidery, it was not surprising that, when I arrived in the U.S., I had with me a large tablecloth decorated with so much embroidery that it could have been a tapestry. It was known as a banquet set, large enough for a dozen place settings, and it was mine to sell. Its price was set at $300, the amount budgeted for my living expenses for the first academic year. The name of a potential buyer, complete with address and phone number, had been given to me before I left China. If I remember correctly, his name was Fairchild and he lived in Tacoma, Washington (adjacent to Seattle).

With the hope of selling the tablecloth to Mr. Fairchild, I had flown to Seattle instead of to San Francisco, the usual route. Unfortunately, Mr. Fairchild was not in town when I called. I was told that he was at the St. Francis Hotel in San Francisco. So I took the train to San Francisco and met him there, where he was staying in the penthouse suite. He took a look at the banquet set, asked the price, and offered to buy it on the spot. He called the appropriate hotel office downstairs and asked for $300 in twenty-dollar bills, which they promptly supplied, and asked me if I would like to stay for lunch. I am not sure whether I was being polite, shy, or afraid that he might change his mind about the tablecloth, but I declined his luncheon invitation. (How I would have enjoyed that lunch!)

Since I was in San Francisco for the evening, I decided to look in the newspaper to see if there were any concerts I might attend. There I saw an announcement for the San Francisco Symphony Orchestra, performing that evening with William Steinberg conducting and Helen Traubel as soprano soloist. Unfortunately, it was sold out. Deciding to try my luck, I went to the concert hall and stood by the box office for about an hour before concert time, hoping for returned tickets, to no avail. However, I did notice that there was a young fellow pacing about with two tickets in his hand. A few minutes after the concert starting time had passed, he came up to me and dejectedly offered me a free ticket, saying something about his date failing to show up. That was how I got to hear the first live performance of a world-class orchestra. What a wonderful welcome to the United States of America!

34

My First Year in the U.S.

After this detour to San Francisco to sell the expensive linen tablecloth, I resumed my intended trip to Indiana, via train, to re-unite with my sister Nancy. Since Nancy was born in Hartford, Connecticut, in 1930, she was a U.S. citizen. She had come to the U.S. the year before to study at Millikin University in Decatur, Illinois, and was staying that summer in Sullivan, Indiana, with the family of Rev. Homer Weisbecker, pastor of the Presbyterian Church in Sullivan. Rev. Weisbecker was my father's old schoolmate and dear friend from their Princeton Seminary days. Since Nancy was in this country without family, Rev. and Mrs. Weisbecker had consented to be her surrogate parents. My short visit there must have been over a weekend, for I was asked to play a piece on the cello for the Sunday morning worship service. That was my first public performance in the U.S.

I arrived at Carroll College in Waukesha, Wisconsin, a week before the fall semester classes began, so as to plan my work/study schedule. Carroll College, a private liberal arts college affiliated with the Presbyterian Church, is the oldest four-year college in Wisconsin. The Wisconsin Territorial Legislature signed the college charter on January 31, 1846, two years before Wisconsin became a state. It was named for Charles Carroll, a signer of the United States Declaration of Independence. Located about ten miles west of Milwaukee, it is now known as Carroll University.

My first impressions of the college were its friendliness, tidiness, and efficiency. It seemed to me as though everyone I had to see was expecting me, starting with the president himself, Dr. Nelson Vance Russell. The next person I saw was the Dean, Dr. John Jansen, who advised me on scholastic matters and what courses to take. Then I met with Mr. Clarence Johnson, the person in charge of the maintenance department, to figure out a regular work schedule of cleaning the library that would not conflict with my class hours. Finally, I had to go to the Music Department to sign up for a practicing schedule. Being part of a small liberal arts college, the Music Department had very few music majors but a fair number of students taking instrumental and voice lessons who needed regular daily practice time and space. Since it was housed in a modest two-story former private home with few practice rooms, the Department had difficulty finding a space where I could practice for three hours each day. Someone came up with the idea that I could have almost unlimited use of the boiler room in the basement of the men's dormitory, if I did not mind sharing it with two weight-lifters. It was a good space, rather spacious, and empty except for an exercise mat, lots of weights, and an occasional weight lifter. So that became my practice studio for the year.

Carroll College was my introduction to ordinary American life. The abundance of food, plentiful milk and Wisconsin cheese, the friendliness of everyone I met – it was an enormous change from wartime in Shanghai. I took my meals with members of the football team, who had also arrived on campus before the semester began. They were, naturally, big guys, who were amazed at the amount of food I could eat and milk I could drink. In the course of the year, thanks to this abundance, I gained back the weight I had lost during the war.

One student in the college was from Liberia – the only black student in the school. After a few weeks he went to the barbershop in town for a haircut but the barber refused to cut his hair. The students in the college were outraged by this refusal and determined that no one would get a haircut until the barber backed down. The boycott was successful and I marveled at American democracy in practice.

The cello professor at Carroll College, Josef Schroetter, was born in Austria in 1891. At the age of 18 he joined the Royal Orchestra of Germany, with whom he toured for the years before World War I. After the war, Schroetter struck out on his own, playing in opera houses and as a soloist with a Swedish orchestra. He emigrated to the U.S. in 1923 and played with the Minneapolis Symphony Orchestra until he moved to Milwaukee in 1927, where he played with the Waukesha Symphony Orchestra and the various predecessors of the Milwaukee Symphony Orchestra. How fortunate I was to have had Mr. Schroetter as my principal teacher and advisor! He was not only a fine cellist and an articulate teacher, but also a kind and generous person, who seemed always to have my wellbeing in mind.

Aside from my cello lessons with Mr. Schroetter, the most significant musical opportunity that Carroll College and Waukesha offered me was the Waukesha Symphony Orchestra, a fine orchestra composed of qualified local players and a core of professional musicians, including Mr. Schroetter, occupying principal positions. The orchestra was led by Milton Weber, an inspiring conductor and violinist from Austria, who also taught at Carroll. It was of a professional standard high enough to perform any major work in the standard orchestral repertoire. To my great surprise, at the first rehearsal of the orchestra I found myself placed at the first stand of the cello section, sitting beside Mr. Schroetter himself. I saw this seating arrangement as a clear indication of his intention to make orchestral playing a serious learning experience and an important part of my studies with him, so I prepared for the weekly orchestra rehearsals as well as I could. This orchestral experience could not have occurred at a better time, for it was a crucial preparation for my musical pursuits the following summer at Tanglewood. So there in Wisconsin I continued to be trained by Germanic musicians, while getting my first taste of a liberal arts education and the American way of life.

At the end of the first semester, Mr. Schroetter and I had a serious discussion about my future studies. He was of the opinion that, if my intention was to make a career in music, I should continue my training in one of the big cities on the east coast and live in a major music center such as New York, Boston, or Philadelphia. With his encouragement and with the concurrence of other friends and relatives whose opinions I respected, I worked hard with Mr. Schroetter to prepare for my relocation east.

The decision for me to attend the New England Conservatory of Music in Boston was not a difficult one to make. It had always been one of the leading music schools in this country and was the one willing to accept me provisionally before my official audition with Samuel Mayes (principal cellist of the Boston Symphony Orchestra at the time) scheduled for late May of 1950. Fortunately, the audition went well and I was admitted to NEC for the fall with a tuition scholarship. Mr. Mayes also recommended me for acceptance with a full scholarship to the Berkshire Music Center at Tanglewood, summer home of the Boston Symphony Orchestra.

CARROLL COLLEGE MUSIC DEPARTMENT
Presents

JOHN HSU

In Cello Recital
Assisted by Carol Gensmer

CHAPEL   7:45 P. M.
_____

PROGRAM

Suite No. 1 in G   Bach
     (for Violoncello only)
          Prelude
          Allemande
          Courante
          Sarabande
          Minuet I and II
          Gigue

Concerto A Minor   Saint Saens
          Allegro non troppo
          Allegretto con moto
          Un peu moins vite — molto Allegro

Waldesruhe (Adagio)   Dvorak
A Dream   Schroetter
Tarantelle   Popper

From a recital program March 23, 1950

38

The Trip East

Between Carroll and Tanglewood, there occurred a memorable travel adventure that was in stark contrast to my air travel from China the year before -- a trip from Milwaukee to Boston with two schoolmates in a rebuilt Model A Ford of uncertain vintage. While my flight on the Stratocruiser represented the speediest and the most comfortable way of traveling at the time, this car adventure gave me a taste of long-distance automobile travel of the 1920s.

This came about as a result of my noticing an ad on the dormitory bulletin board from a graduating senior seeking someone to share the driving and the cost of his return trip home to Boston. His name was Joseph Pynchon. I got in touch with him first by phone and then found him at the dormitory parking lot where he was re-building the engine of his Model A. We made sure that the car had enough room to take my cello and luggage before agreeing upon our intended departure date and time.

To our surprise, near departure time, there was another graduating senior, Oliver Strom from Milwaukee, who wanted to come along, just for fun. In order to accommodate Ollie, we had to take out the back seat and replace it with my steamer trunk, which needless to say was not as comfortable. To be fair, we agreed upon a rotating seating system, which gave each of us an equal amount of time on the hard, uncomfortable trunk/seat. We also agreed beforehand that, in order to save money, we would avoid staying in hotels on the way. We took along jungle hammocks, which we were able to string up at night between large trees off the highway that were strong and close enough together. We also made plentiful sandwiches with leftovers from the final dormitory lunch to take along for the road. Alas, we had to discard our provisions on the second day, due to spoilage, so we ended up eating at diners for most of the five-day journey.

In spite of its age, the Model 'A' served us well, except for its tendency to boil over on steep hills, especially going up the Taconic Trail in Massachusetts. Whenever that happened, we had to wait for the radiator to cool and refill it before continuing the drive. Nevertheless, it was inexpensive and fun. We ended the journey by driving onto the campus of Wellesley College to show off the car, attracting the admiration of the co-eds. What a grand finale it was! Ollie had such a thrill that he bought the car from Joe and drove back to Milwaukee alone.

With the Tanglewood season following soon after my arrival in Boston, I had to do a lot of cello practicing immediately, so did not have time to look for a place to live in Boston. Realizing that there would be a couple of unoccupied bedrooms in her house after Joe went off to teach in Illinois in the fall, Mrs. Pynchon very kindly offered me the use of one of them when I returned to Boston from Tanglewood in late August. Thus I became her tenant for most of my first year in Boston. I was especially grateful to her for her generous offer because, as I had no car, her home was the ideal place for me to begin my life in Boston. Conveniently situated in Newton Highlands, it was near the Woodward and Elliot Street bus stop of the B&W bus line, which also had a bus stop right in front of the New England Conservatory after a 20-minute ride.

Tanglewood Music Center

Serge Koussevitzky founded what was then known as the Berkshire Music Center in 1940 to allow emerging professional performers, conductors, and composers to hone their skills with musicians of the Boston Symphony Orchestra in a summer program in a beautiful setting. For me it was also an opportunity to assess my progress toward becoming a professional musician.

Tanglewood was a veritable paradise. For eight full weeks, every waking hour was devoted to music. For the first time in my life I had the privilege of meeting, hearing, and learning from great artists and leading figures in the world of music, as well as making music with my contemporaries from across the country and abroad. Many of them were already professionals; all were tireless in their pursuit of excellence. Sixty-five years later, recalling that summer is still a source of inspiration for me. Never again in my life did I play so much great music with so many fine musicians in such a short period of time.

During the initial days of the festival I awaited, with great suspense and a certain amount of anxiety, for the announcement of the assignments, concert dates, and rehearsal schedules for the performing groups, as well as the names of the performers and the coach for each group.

The resident composer that summer was Jacques Ibert from France, whose music was one of the main features of the festival. I had not played his music before, so I welcomed the opportunity to become acquainted with it. I was very pleased that I was assigned to perform his Trio for harp, violin, and cello, with his harpist-daughter Jacqueline Ibert-Gillet and violinist Diana Steiner, to be coached by him and BSO harpist Bernard Zighera. I was also assigned to be the principal cellist of the orchestra for the performance of his opera *Le Roi d'Yvetot*, with conductor Jan Popper. Other chamber music works to which I was assigned for performance were Brahms Quintet, Op. 111, and Beethoven String Quartet, Op. 18, No. 2, both to be coached by William Kroll of the Kroll String Quartet.

The curious cellist

The most adventuresome of my chamber music experiences was
studying and playing (but without performance) Schoenberg's Third
Quartet with Eugen Lehner (violist of the Kolisch Quartet that
championed the work from the time of its appearance in 1927) himself as
violist and coach. How lucky it was that in Shanghai I had learned a bit
about Schoenberg's twelve-tone technique from Mr. Schloss!

The Tanglewood Orchestra was scheduled to play several works under
various conductors during the course of the summer, reaching a climax
with the performance of Tchaikovsky's Symphony No. 4 conducted by
Serge Koussevitsky. And a musical climax it was indeed! Playing under
the legendary Koussevitsky was an indescribable experience. Even
though he was inspiring and meticulous during rehearsals, at the concert
he exuded an additional electric force that inspired the players anew with
greater expressivity, spontaneity, power and abandon. It was the first
time that I took part in an ecstatic orchestral performance.

The New England Conservatory

It was with great anticipation that I arrived at the New England Conservatory on the first day of registration in the fall semester of 1950. The first order of business was to take an advanced placement test for music theory with Chester Williams of the theory faculty, in order to determine the equivalency of what I had learned on the subject in Shanghai, so as to avoid redundancies in my course selection. Based on the result of the test, I was given enough advanced placement credits in theory courses that, together with course credits transferred from Carroll College to satisfy certain academic requirements, I was able to join the class of 1953 without difficulty and continue with a lighter than usual class schedule.

This reduced course load meant that I was able to take on more chamber music activities than were required, as well as to work as piano accompanist in the studio of Frederick Jagel, the Chairman of the Voice Department. This gave me not only the opportunity to learn something of the vocal repertoire but also another way to earn some money. Being a piano accompanist in this capacity meant being able to follow the singer's lead, playing many notes as expressively as possible with as little ego as possible.

All the faculty members with whom I came into contact inspired in me a desire to delve further into the subject matter at hand. In addition to my cello teachers, the two who influenced me the most were Francis Judd Cooke and Chester Williams, who instilled in me a lasting sense of musical curiosity. They were truly my mentors and became my life-long friends.

In spite of Mr. Mayes' support and encouragement enabling me to attend Tanglewood, I awaited my first cello lesson with him with a certain amount of anxiety. I had heard by then that in the previous couple of years, he taught only one cello student each year, and that I was his chosen student that academic year. Knowing that, I began the year working as hard as I could, but by the end of the first semester found myself slowed down by bursitis. Thereafter, I made uneven progress in my lessons depending on the state of my shoulder.

By the end of the second semester, I was totally incapacitated by bursitis. Despite having cortisone shots and physical therapy, I had to stop playing This disaster shook me to the core. That summer was the most discouraging and worrisome time of my life hitherto.

While I was trying to cope with this setback, Mr. Mayes announced that, due to his busy performance and recording schedule for the following year, he would not be able to take on any student at NEC. He recommended that I study with Alfred Zighera, who was the principal teacher of all the other cello majors, and I followed his advice.

Mr. Zighera had been the Assistant Principal cellist of the Boston Symphony since 1925, when Serge Koussevitsky became conductor of the orchestra. Trained at the national conservatory in Paris, he won its first prize in cello by unanimous vote in 1915, when he was only seventeen. Subsequently, he became first cellist both in the *Société des concert de Conservatoire* and in Koussevitsky's orchestra in Paris.

In retrospect, this change of teacher was beneficial to me at the time both in terms of physical recovery and musical development. Mr. Zighera's bowing technique and playing style were more relaxed and less demanding of the shoulder, so speeded my recovery from bursitis. His emphasis on developing the versatility of the lower half of the bow helped me to increase its expressive capability and to broaden its range of tonal inflection. I felt that I was learning so much from Mr. Zighera that I continued to work with him for my remaining four years at NEC.

That depressing spring semester of 1951 was brightened unexpectedly by Harrison Keller, President of the Conservatory, who offered me the use of a fine antique Italian cello that had recently been given to the Conservatory by the Crowninshield Estate in Salem, Massachusetts for the purpose of lending to deserving cellists who would benefit from the advantages of playing on such an instrument. It was attributed to a lesser-known member of the legendary Guarneri family – an instrument such that I never would have dreamt of possessing.

I found myself in a strange emotional state. I felt that I had failed but nonetheless been rewarded. My playing was curtailed but I had been lent a beautiful instrument. I fell in love with this cello immediately. Not only were its sound and appearance so incredibly beautiful, but it also spoke with ease and spontaneity whatever I wanted it to say. It taught me how to be a better player for the next four and a half years that it was mine to use.

The cello I had been using was one I had bought in Shanghai. At that time I needed something better than the one I had borrowed from a friend to start on, and this one was affordable and in good playing condition. I was told that it was a German cello, maker unknown. Going from this decent but nondescript instrument to the subtle and eloquent Guarneri was like going from a Jeep to a BMW.

My five years in Boston were full of marvels. Within the Conservatory was Jordan Hall, one of the finest concert halls in the world, especially for chamber music and recitals. Not only did the students have the opportunity to hear great performances by famous artists in this acoustically superb concert venue, we also had the privilege of rehearsing and performing there ourselves. One block away from the Conservatory was Symphony Hall, home of the incomparable Boston Symphony Orchestra, where we listened with admiration and disbelief almost every Friday afternoon, after rushing over to line up in front of the box office to get the cheap seats, or sometimes to be sneaked in by some friendly ushers. Then there were the two great museums within a short walk from the Conservatory: The Boston Museum of Art and the Isabella Stewart Gardner Museum. Within these surroundings I indulged myself in all that was beautiful and uplifting in music and art, sometimes to the point of being oblivious to the real world beyond.

Another advantage of living in Boston that soon became apparent was the number of freelance orchestral engagements that were available to me in the city and its vicinity, as well as in other New England cities within commuting distance from Boston.

When I arrived in the fall of 1950, I became the assistant principal cellist of the Springfield Symphony Orchestra in Springfield, Massachusetts, in which position I remained for five years. The following year I joined the Rhode Island Philharmonic Orchestra in Providence. Thereafter I also played with Boris Goldovsky's New England Opera Company and the Handel and Haydn Society Orchestra in the city, the Worcester Symphony Orchestra nearby, and the distant Portland Symphony Orchestra in Portland, Maine.

All these gigs not only enlarged my orchestral repertoire, but also sharpened my sight-reading ability, a basic requisite for a freelance musician. In addition, there were opportunities for solo and chamber music performances at churches and synagogues on festive and celebratory occasions, and appearances in various concert series in museums and other concert venues. During my years as a graduate student, I was also the cello instructor at Phillips Academy in Andover, and in the Newton Public Schools. So my five exciting years in Boston (1950-55) passed very quickly, and gave me plentiful musical satisfaction.

During my student years I lived with friends in apartments that were affordable for those of us with minimal resources. I spent two years with an oboist and a music education major, veterans studying at the Conservatory on the G. I. bill. The ex-Navy guy cleaned (swabbed!), the other guy did the dishes, and I cooked. Buying only items that were on sale, we each managed to eat for $1.00 a day and I became a specialist in meals that were very quick and easy to prepare.

One day I got a message that the president of the university wanted to see me. With some trepidation I went to his office and learned that a letter had come, addressed to:

John Hsu
Student
U.S.A.
Personal and Urgent

Thanks to a central office (in Chicago?), that kept a registry of the 4,000 or so Chinese students in the U.S., the letter had reached me. It contained the welcome news that my parents, still in Communist China, were OK— news I was very glad to get. I only regret that I neglected to keep the envelope!

In the midst of my hectic life as a professional freelance musician/cello instructor/final-year graduate student, I got married on November 7, 1954. My wife, Ursula Dorge, was a linguist who had just immigrated to the U.S. from Germany, where she had been a translator/interpreter for the Office of the U.S. High Commissioner. We discovered from the start

With Ursula

that we enjoyed each other's company and had much in common. As was the case with many Germans, Ursula had appreciated music from childhood. She was a professional, independent, and sympathetic woman, and took the uncertain future of a young musician in stride. Having also lived through WWII and its resultant deprivations, we shared our frugal habits with ease. Most comforting of all, our marriage dispelled our loneliness.

It was a sheer stroke of luck that just as I was completing my graduate studies and in the midst of preparing for job hunting, Cornell University announced its intention to appoint a cello instructor to begin in the fall of 1955. With encouragement and strong support from Chester Williams, who had become the Dean of the Conservatory in 1951, and my other teachers, I applied for the position and was invited to Ithaca for an interview. Of this interview, I remember little except that it took place at noon, after a grueling two-day, approximately 13-hour drive from Boston. (Before the building of the Massachusetts Turnpike and the New York Thruway, such a trip meant driving mostly on Rt. 9 and a bit on Rt. 2 in Massachusetts, and mostly on Rt. 20 and an hour on Rt. 13 in New York.)

Unexpectedly, I had to drive non-stop back to Boston after the interview because when I arrived in Ithaca that morning, I received word that my wife had just had a miscarriage and was in the hospital. After all these years, the only memory of the interview that I can recall now with certainty is that I was offered the job, and I accepted it.

Before going to Cornell I spent a few summers at Camp Walt Whitman, in New Hampshire. As Director of Music, my responsibilities included conducting an orchestra in which every girl or boy who wanted to, could play. Some children were already quite advanced on their instruments; others were barely more than beginners. I wrote parts especially tailored to each child's ability so all could participate. The young flutist who could play only a few notes, the trombonist whose arms were still too short to reach the farthest position on the instrument, the accomplished violinist – all were accommodated. This was an interesting challenge that resulted in many happy children and many grateful parents, one of whom slipped me a tip with his goodbye handshake!

This camp was where I learned to swim, never having had the opportunity before. And it was also where I broke my leg, sliding into third base in a softball game. The ride to Dartmouth-Hitchcock Medical Center in the back of a station wagon was excruciatingly painful but the doctors were excellent. With five screws they fastened a metal plate in my leg that I have to this day. The break was so bad that it took eleven months in a cast for the bones to heal. Consequently I spent my first year at Cornell on crutches.

In Boston

Cornell University

Ithaca is gorges, and Ithaca is gorgeous! It also has beautiful hills, Cayuga Lake, and most welcoming of all, the Cornell campus.

In 1955, the Music Department was housed in a three-story, formerly one-family house on Wait Avenue, near a big women's dormitory called Balch Hall, across Triphammer Bridge from the Arts Quad. When I drove onto campus for the first time, the directions I had in hand led me to believe that Balch Hall was the home of the Music Department. I was duly impressed, until I went inside and was directed to the small house around the corner.

In this modest accommodation was a small music department with a distinguished faculty, chaired by Donald J. Grout, one of the leading musicologists of the time. Author of the popular A History of Western Music, Grout was among the first musician-scholars in this country to reflect upon and write about historical performance practice. It was my good fortune to learn some of his views when I joined the Cornell music faculty.

Other senior faculty members included the composer Robert Palmer (at Cornell since 1943), pianist John Kirkpatrick (since 1946), musicologist William Austin (since 1947), and conductor/violinist Robert Hull (since 1946). The newest addition to the faculty was Karel Husa, the Czech composer from Paris, who had arrived in 1954. Working amongst these productive musicians was a constant source of inspiration, for they were full of ideas for teaching and for concerts.

Having long before sold the cello I had brought from Shanghai, I accepted the job at Cornell without actually owning an instrument! Fortunately, a dear friend's mother was considering selling hers, which she kindly did for a price that I could afford at that moment. It was an anonymous 18th century French cello with a sweet and appealing sound. With this instrument I played the first performance in the U.S. of the *Ballade* for cello and small orchestra by the Dutch composer Frank Martin at the Cornell Festival of Contemporary Arts on April 15, 1956.

This performance made me realize that for future concerto performances with large orchestra accompaniment I would need to have a cello with a larger tone. Fortuitously, such a cello was put on sale the following year in the liquidation of an estate in the adjacent city of Cortland, NY. The price was right, but again it was an instrument by an anonymous maker. Limited by my financial resources, I had unintentionally become a collector of anonymous cellos, owning in sequence three such instruments.

View of Cayuga Lake from the Cornell campus

The Viola da Gamba

One day in 1957, during an informal discussion on whether the department should form a Collegium Musicum of period instruments for the performance of early music, Donald Grout asked me whether I would be willing to learn to play the viola da gamba if the university were to provide the instrument. Being young and foolhardy, I said yes, without thinking about the investment of time required or assessing the chance of success while my time was preoccupied performing as a cellist and teaching cello and theory.

Although I do not recall subsequent discussions on the subject, he must have considered my response as a positive commitment on my part and soon thereafter secured the necessary funds (only $804!) to order a chest of viols (viola da gambas) -- a treble, a tenor, and a bass -- complete with bows and cases, from the German viol maker Eugen Sprenger of Frankfurt.

I had almost forgotten about this conversation when, one day in the spring of 1960, a huge wooden box from Germany arrived at the Music Department with my name on it. So now it was my turn to make good on my end of the bargain, and I set out immediately to teach myself how to play this instrument. With my full schedule of teaching and performing during the academic year, it was difficult to find time to work on one more musical instrument, so I had to wait patiently for the summer months to devote myself to mastering the viol.

The term "viol" is a generic one that applies to all the different sizes of this family of bowed stringed instruments that preceded the violin family. Unlike the violin family, in which each member has a different name -- violin, viola, cello, and contrabass -- the viol family designates different sizes by an additional adjective: treble, alto, tenor, or bass. The viol family members commonly had six strings. As its Italian name *viola da gamba* (*gamba* means leg) suggests, the instrument is held vertically between the legs.

Viols were popular primarily in ensemble playing during the 16th and 17th centuries. In 17th century England, playing in an ensemble of three to six or more viols was so popular that all the best composers of the time composed music for viol consorts, as they were called. However, various styles of solo playing also developed in different countries.

Impatient to find out what new musical experiences were awaiting me with this new instrument, I decided to schedule my first viola da gamba recital on Monday, April 10, 1961. In this endeavor, I received a most unexpected but welcome source of support from the new department chair, William Austin, who was an accomplished keyboard player versed in basso continuo realization. Although an expert on 20th century music, he offered his collaboration as harpsichordist so we could explore the viability of viola da gamba recitals.

In the early 1960s, viols were heard infrequently in concerts. Their rare appearances were usually in one of two guises: as a single bass viol playing a continuo part of a baroque work with a keyboard instrument, or in a consort of three or more viols or mixed instruments. No one in this country had yet specialized in playing the viola da gamba as a solo instrument, and the solo viol music heard in concerts at this time was most often German in origin – sonatas by J. S. Bach, Telemann, Handel, and other, lesser-known German composers. During the summer of 1960 and the following academic year, Bill Austin and I learned this limited repertoire of German gamba sonatas, along with a few modest collections of French viol pieces available only in questionable editions.

My first solo program consisted of solo sonatas by Handel, Telemann, and Bach as well as pieces by Tobias Hume. With this debut recital, I was smitten by the intimate and gentle "tone of voice" of this historic musical instrument.

Many colleges in New York State were interested in having a musical novelty such as a viola da gamba recital in their concert series. At times the local press was not prepared to deal with it. One announcement in 1961 had me playing the "ulola da garnba," and "vlola da ganba." A

Binghamton (N.Y.) *Sun-Bulletin* notice was quoted in *The New Yorker* of November 16, 1963:

> "Other concerts, all at the Harpur College Theater, are slated as follows: Nov. 18 at 8:15 P.M., a recital by Viola Da Gamba on the harpsichord, with John Hsu and Rudolph Kremer."

Viola da gamba recital with Rudolph Kremer

In the process of imagining programming possibilities, it occurred to me that if we could program a mixed recital of solo viol music with harpsichord accompaniment in the first half and romantic sonatas for cello and piano, such as those by Rachmaninoff and Chopin, for the second half of the program, we could then dispense with the verbal descriptions we felt obliged to offer the audience to explain the differences between viola da gamba and the cello, the music written for them, and the different musical worlds that they represented. This kind of mixed recital program proved very popular, but the necessity of carrying two big instruments required travel logistics that were too cumbersome for long-term endeavors.

But one such concert in particular gave me special satisfaction. It took place in the Memorial Center in Milwaukee on March 31, 1963. Milton Weber, conductor of the Waukesha Symphony Orchestra and a professor at Carroll College when I was a freshman there, was now also conductor of the Music for Youth Chamber Orchestra in Milwaukee. Having heard that I was concertizing with the viola da gamba, he invited me to play with his chamber orchestra of talented young musicians. For that occasion, I proposed the pairing of the Viola da Gamba Concerto in D major by Giuseppe Tartini (1692-1770) with the Elegy for Cello and Orchestra by Gabriel Fauré (1845-1924). The latter, a fine example of pre-Wagnerian romanticism expressed by the familiar rich tone of the cello, was an ideal musical contrast to the elegance of the Tartini concerto, thus highlighting the characteristics and merits of the unfamiliar viola da gamba. After learning so much from playing with Milton Weber and the Waukesha Symphony Orchestra in 1949-50, I was pleased that I had the opportunity to offer something unique and worthwhile to him and the Milwaukee/Waukesha musicians and concert audience.

The Tecchler Cello

A serious string player needs a good instrument as a collaborator. My three barely adequate anonymous cellos had served me well, but could neither teach me anything about making music nor allow me to express myself in any subtle way. By 1962-63 I was resigned to the prospect of never owning a truly wonderful cello.

Then came a miracle. Following Mr. Weber's invitation to play with his Music for Youth Orchestra in Milwaukee, Mr. Schroetter, my teacher at Carroll College, wrote to offer me the use of his cello for the concert, a superb Italian instrument made by David Tecchler in Rome in 1711. (Among precious cellos, a Tecchler is ranked second only to a Stradivarius.) Soon after the concert, Mr. Schroetter telephoned to say that since he was retiring soon, and his Tecchler and I seemed to match so compatibly, he would like very much for me to be its next owner. To make that possible, he offered to sell it to me for the same price that he had paid in 1938.

With this demonstration of generosity and deep friendship, my frustration with uninspiring anonymous cellos became a thing of the past. From then until arthritis put a stop to my playing, I enjoyed every moment I put my bow on the Tecchler. What musical bliss it was during the 35 years we spent together! I never ceased to admire its eloquence and easy delivery. I am forever grateful to Mr. Schroetter for his noble deed, and have established a permanent scholarship fund at Carroll University in his memory: The Schroetter/Hsu Endowed Scholarship.

Imagine what a terrible moment it was when I realized that I would have to be separated from this source of constant inspiration, which had become so much a part of my life! Of course selling it outright crossed my mind, but I wanted to perpetuate Mr. Schroetter's generosity and acknowledge his immense contribution to the joys and successes of my musical life. Remembering how the New England Conservatory's fine old Italian cello had helped me during my student days, I decided to donate the Tecchler to the conservatory so that future deserving cello students there would have the opportunity to develop their art and expand their musical imagination by learning from, and being inspired by, the inexplicable magic of playing the Tecchler. So to NEC it went, in 1999.

By now it has already benefitted many aspiring young cellists. It gave me special satisfaction to know that the privilege of using the Tecchler in the academic year 2011-2012 was awarded to a deserving Chinese cellist from Shanghai.

The Tecchler cello

Laurence Lesser, cellist at New England Conservatory,
receiving the Tecchler cello in 1999

French Viol Music, Background

The French solo viol tradition reached its apex in France by the late 17th century, and the bass viol became a virtuoso instrument in the hands of 18th century experts who were player-composers. They spawned a whole new genre of exquisite solo viol music that is unlike any music composed elsewhere in Europe at any time.

The leading member of this group of player-composers was Marin Marais (1656-1728), who was also the most prolific composer of music for viols. He composed over 600 pieces, 559 of them for solo viol and continuo. (Continuo is the shortened term for *basso continuo*, which means a continuous bass part with figures indicating the harmonic content of the music. This bass part is usually played by a harpsichord or lute, with or without an accompanying bass viol.)

It was said at the time that while Marais played like an angel, Antoine Forqueray (1672-1745) played like the devil. Forqueray's extant works in the *Bibliothèque nationale* comprise five suites of solo pieces with accompaniment that represent the most technically advanced and difficult music for the instrument, full of chordal textures that require frequent multiple-stopping, and richly ornamented melodic lines that call for great agility.

In their compositions, we can see reflections of their musical personalities and their contrasting musical temperaments. We encounter two extraordinarily inventive composers who were keen on exploring and expanding the range of musical possibilities of the solo viol. Marais reached more often for better realization of lyricism in viol playing through more subtle and sensitive scansion of imagined poetic lines. Forqueray, on the other hand, seemed to concentrate on exploring the instrumental limits of chordal sonorities in solo viol playing. Both conveyed their musical intentions through the fingerings and bowings provided in the music.

While looking in the Cornell Music Library for gamba music, I soon realized that there was a scarcity of published music written for solo viol and also of historical instructional sources for playing it. I had already been carried away by the extraordinary music of Marais and Forqueray, and I was impatient to play it. With my timely promotion to Associate Professor of Music with permanent tenure at Cornell in 1962, I decided to devote my sabbatical leave in the fall of 1964 to investigating the French solo viol repertoire of the 17th and 18th centuries.

I had an ambitious goal for my sabbatical leave: not only to become acquainted with the entire French solo viol repertoire but also to find treatises and other documents of the time that would explain the virtuoso technique necessary to play this incomparable music. I knew that recapturing a historically valid style of playing would involve understanding the musical rhetoric and aesthetics of the period. The collection at the *Bibliothèque Nationale* was clearly the place to start.

Fortunately, the International Musicological Society was meeting that year in Salzburg, Austria, and my colleague Donald Grout was its president. We both had planned to attend the IMS meeting, and he generously offered to take advantage of the occasion to introduce me to musicians and scholars who held important posts in the various libraries and other Parisian institutions where I intended to do my research. Thus doors were opened and the way paved for my work in Paris from September to December, 1964.

In Europe, 1964

In 1964, the National Library of France on rue Richelieu had just built a new building across the street for its Music Department. Into this new and spacious place, it brought together the two main music collections in Paris, its own and that of the *Conservatoire de Musique*, thus facilitating research work for its users. Surrounded by this vast and priceless collection of historical musical sources, and assisted by a helpful library staff, I became acquainted with an unexpectedly large amount of solo music for the viol by French composers of the 17th and 18th centuries. I was able to study the complete instrumental works of Marin Marais and his contemporaries from manuscripts and/or their original publications. I felt like a kid in a candy store! It was a very fruitful four months of exciting work.

I recall two conversations with François Lesure, soon to be Chief of the Music Department of the *Bibliothèque* Nationale, when I came across the music of Louis de Caix d'Hervelois (ca. 1680 - ca. 1755). First, I had no idea how to pronounce the name, and was told that "Caix" should be pronounced like "Aix" in Aix-en-Provence, with an initial "k" and a final "x".

The second conversation caused me some embarrassment at the time, but might actually have served to make him aware of what I was doing in the library every day. Since my goal was to get acquainted as soon as possible with as much solo viol music as possible, I copied and scored, on the spot, all the works that I wanted to learn immediately.

It so happened that when I came to the music of de Caix, I ran out of the extra large music paper that I had brought along. Not wanting to interrupt my progress and shop for paper at that time, I went to Mr. Lesure's office to ask if he had any that I could borrow.

That thoughtless question of mine set off such a prolonged paper hunt that all I wished for then was to be invisible. Eventually he found two sheets of old and discolored but still blank staff paper and gave them to me with the courteous apology that he wished he had something better. From then on, he began to show keen interest in what I was doing.

As a result of the intensive work I did there, I returned home with the largest microfilm collection of French solo viol music in the U.S., which I gave to the Cornell Music Library. I also gathered a sufficient number of manuscripts and early publications of treatises on the playing technique of the time, which enabled me to write <u>A Handbook of French Baroque Viol Technique</u> in 1981.

Rue Bertin Poirée, the street in Paris where Marais lived for a time

Personal Transitions

In 1967, I was appointed Chairman of the Department of Music at Cornell University. It should have been a time of contentment, but it was not. All was not well, because it coincided with the low point of my wife's professional career. Ursula had been teaching German in the Language Department for some time as a native speaker, and had just lost her job due to a run-in with the senior professor of the course regarding his choice of teaching material. This incident in a college town like Ithaca pretty much foreclosed any further employment opportunities in language teaching, which she enjoyed. When we first arrived in Ithaca, Ursula worked as a department secretary in two different academic departments at Cornell for 3-4 years. She found that sort of work uninteresting and could not imagine doing it for any length of time. So at the height of my professional satisfaction, she was at her lowest.

In retrospect, there is no question that I was not enough of a sympathetic and understanding husband under the circumstances. With all my new administrative responsibilities, I am sure that I was impatient and unavailable for any extended discussion. We both knew that there was nothing in Ithaca that would give her a lifetime of professional satisfaction. From that moment on, our twelve-year-old marriage began to fall apart quickly, and we were divorced the following year. Ursula left Ithaca and ultimately worked in the State Department in Washington, DC, until her retirement. She died in 2008.

Nineteen sixty-seven and early 1968 was a period of indescribably hard work, which, in fact, did provide some degree of solace, and made me less aware of my loneliness and fatigue. My European concert tours in February of 1967 and January of 1968 also gave me considerable professional satisfaction, with recitals and radio recordings taking me to London, Newcastle, Edinburgh, Brussels, Berlin, and Zürich. However, there were moments when I wondered how much longer I could keep up the pretense of normalcy. Then one day late in 1967, Cupid decided to shoot his arrow at me, and I was saved by love. I do not remember now on what day and at what time it happened, but I do remember the place and the circumstance.

In our relatively new music building at the heart of the Arts College Quad, I had an office conveniently located next to the Music Library, with a water fountain right outside my office door. One afternoon I stepped out of my office to get a drink of water and ran into a familiar young woman, who gave me the most beautiful smile I had seen in a long time. In fact, I remembered that smile as a familiar one from a year or two ago when she was a graduate student working part-time in the Music Library. So I said something like, "I am glad that you are back."

That unpremeditated word of welcome must have touched her. She explained that she had indeed been away for over a year to get her graduate degree in library science at the University of Michigan in Ann Arbor, and had just returned to work in the Cornell Library. I could not remember her name and was too embarrassed to ask, so after she left, I went to ask the Music Librarian, who was my best friend, for her name and phone number.

Impatient as always, I called her immediately and invited her to dinner at The Station, a cozy restaurant in the discarded and renovated former railway station. We had a delightful time together that evening, and that delightful time has continued to this day. We were married on July 31, 1968, and we have shared an exciting and rich life together ever since.

My wife, Martha Russell, was born in Wheeling, WV, across the Ohio River from her hometown of Shadyside, Ohio. Having played piano and French horn, she initially majored in music at The College of Wooster, but after a summer in Vienna, Austria, participating in the first year of the "Wooster in Vienna" program, she changed her major to German. A year in Germany after graduation led to graduate work at Cornell University, where she earned her M.A in German Literature with a minor in music history.

As fate would have it, she had a summer job as a student assistant in the Music Library next to my office. It would be two more years before we actually had a conversation, but seeds were sown at that time. Her love of music, and particularly of my music-making, has brought us both a lot of pleasure over the years.

Martha is my ideal soul mate, my lover, my confidant, my best friend, the most trustworthy critic and loyal supporter of all my musical endeavors. She was always there -- proof reading the first volumes of the Marais edition with the original part books on one side and my scoring of the music on the other; sitting in on almost all of my recordings, making notes on each "take" and being sure all the music was covered; listening for balance before concerts; page-turning when necessary; keeping our harpsichord in tune; and once even accompanying me on the harpsichord for a performance of a Marais *Tombeau* during a lecture. She has been my perfect partner in our life together for the past 47 years, adapting easily and graciously to whatever unusual situations arose.

With Martha, 1974

With Martha, 1994

With Martha, 2014

Playing Beethoven with Rudolf Kolisch

In 1967 when I became Department Chairman, the first person I wanted to invite to Cornell as a guest was Rudolf Kolisch, the founder and first violinist of the Kolisch Quartet. In the 1920's this quartet was known for being a champion of "modernist" music, primarily that of Schoenberg, Berg and Bartok. But my primary interest had been sparked by his two articles in *The Musical Quarterly*, vol. XXIX, Nos. 2 and 3, April and July of 1943: "Tempo and Character in Beethoven's Music – Part I and Part II." I asked him to come perform a program of chamber music by Beethoven with our performing faculty members. The featured work was to be the String Quartet, Op. 132, with David Montague, violin, George Green, viola, and myself on the cello.

Kolisch believed that the musical goals presented by Beethoven were the actual wishes of the composer and therefore worthy of respect without compromise on the part of the performer. The performance, given March 10, 1968, was revelatory in that many of the doubtful tempi that Beethoven proposed were not only musically feasible, but at times even helpful to the performer. I still treasure the memory of this collaboration, which Kolisch happily called "fruitful." When he left, he gave me the score from which he had performed -- a miniature score cut up and pasted on a large piece of stiff paper. The clear implication was that he had just given his last performance of this Beethoven quartet.

Antoine Forqueray

When I returned to Ithaca in 1965 with my treasure trove of solo works for the viola da gamba, I was impatient to learn to play the works of one player-composer in particular, those of Antoine Forqueray (1672-1745). It was said that his five suites had not been played in their entirety in modern times. Thus I encountered a challenge that I could not resist: to master all five suites in time to perform them in 1972, the year of the tercentenary of the composer's birth.

If it were not for the fingerings provided by his son, some of his pieces might have been disregarded in the course of time as unplayable. These fingerings were what encouraged me not to give up. What they said to me was that with them the music is playable, provided that the fingers suggested were placed in the right sequence. Therein lay the tricks of the trade.

For reasons I cannot now remember, in the process of learning these suites I chose to begin with the fourth one, and included it in the program when I was invited to perform at the Royal College of Music in London and at a private concert in Brussels, Belgium, accompanied by Layton Ring in 1966. It was at this private concert that I met Pierre Gorlé, owner of the Belgian recording company *Disques Alpha*, who offered to issue an LP of this unusual music under his label.

For this LP, I chose to record Forqueray's Suite No. 4 in G Minor and the Suite No. 3 in D Minor by Louis de Caix d'Hervelois. I felt that the fiery and intense virtuoso music of Forqueray and the intimate and lyrical music of de Caix d'Hervelois would enhance the individuality of each composer. The accompaniment for this LP was played by my Cornell colleague William Austin on the harpsichord, and Barbara Mueser on the viol. The disc was released in 1968.

Shortly after making this recording, I ordered a seven-string instrument, necessary for playing French solo viol music, from Günter Hellwig in Lübeck. I had hoped to get it early in 1971 so that I would have ample time to prepare to use it for the recording of all five Forqueray suites planned for March of 1972. As it turned out, the instrument did not reach me until near the time of the recording, but I used it nevertheless. The five suites were recorded by The Musical Heritage Society and released later in 1972, in time for the tercentenary. The formidable Louis Bagger played the harpsichord. The continuo viol part was superbly played by the late Gian Lyman Silbiger. This recording was made possible by a grant by The Hull Memorial Publication Fund of Cornell University. In 2014, Martha arranged to have it put on YouTube.

"La Rameau" from an early edition of Forqueray's music

Performances in Germany and the Netherlands

Pierre Gorlé, owner of the Belgian recording company *Disques Alpha,* whom I had met in Belgium in 1966, must have done a good job of distributing the LP in Europe, for I began to receive invitations for recitals and radio broadcast recordings. European radio stations differed from ours in that, in addition to broadcasting music available on commercial LPs (now CDs), major European radio stations in big cities also engaged musicians to record particular compositions that had not yet been recorded commercially, in order to broaden the scope of their musical offerings.

Here is an example of the seriousness and alertness with which a German radio station kept up with the job of programming. One day soon after the release of my LP, I received an invitation from the Berlin Free Radio (*Sender Freies Berlin)* to record at their studio other solo works for the gamba besides those on the LP. My acceptance led not only to a recording there in 1968, but also to numerous other recordings for various German radio stations during the next decade. Again I had the good fortune of having a fine harpsichordist as collaborator. Ulrich

Bremsteller, who accompanied me in Berlin, and I were so musically compatible that he became my accompanist for all my subsequent radio recordings and recitals in Germany.

Ulrich Bremsteller and his children, 1972

The initial Berlin radio recording led to engagements at the *Amerika Haus* in Berlin, which invited me to play a recital there the following year when I returned for a repeat engagement at the Berlin Free Radio.

This in turn led to other America House concerts in Germany, and to concerts at museums with famous historical musical instrument collections. Noteworthy among them were the concert and recording of the three Sonatas for Viola da Gamba and Harpsichord by J.S. Bach, performed in collaboration with the distinguished Canadian harpsichordist Kenneth Gilbert at the *Germanisches Nationalmuseum Nürnberg*, using the museum's historical instruments. That performance was recorded by Da Camera Records of Germany and released as an LP in 1971.

These recordings and concerts also led to numerous engagements in the Netherlands, where I had the pleasure of collaborating for several years with the marvelous Dutch harpsichordist Marijke Smit Sibinga, both in recordings and in concerts, including one at the famed *Gemeentemuseum* in The Hague, in which we played their historical instruments.

With Marijke Smit Sibinga in Amsterdam

The America Houses in Berlin and in other German cities were established by the American government following the end of the Second World War to provide an opportunity for German citizens to learn more about American culture and politics. They were the foundation of what some later called the "Marshall Plan of Ideas" – a U.S. public diplomacy initiative that set a standard for later programs around the world. Thus, all the presentations at the America House were meant to help enhance the image of the USA and improve the relationship between the two countries. With that in mind, I derived not only musical pleasure from my America House concerts, but also some satisfaction knowing that I was contributing, albeit in a very small way, to the realization of the peaceful goal of our country's foreign policy.

The following quote from the newspaper review of my America House recital in Frankfurt is an example of one discriminating listener's account.

Excerpt from *Frankfurter Allgemeine*, January 10, 1970:

From time to time the America House presents, in its varied cultural programs, chamber music evenings of special sophistication, such as are scarcely to be heard in any other venue in Frankfurt. They are announced as "Concerts for gourmets" in the monthly program. A little more than a year ago Joan Benson presented an evening of clavichord music by various composers in the Bach family. And now we got to hear a whole evening of pure gamba music, accompanied by the harpsichord. One could get the impression that the America House wanted to demonstrate that the USA not only had astronauts and first class symphony orchestras, that it was not only the cradle of pop-art and underground film…but also that it wished to surpass European standards and possibilities in the practice of historical music performance…Hsu's gamba playing is colorful in every respect – articulation – phrasing – and particularly in ornamentation.

Performances in the United Kingdom

In 1966, I was invited by Natalie Dolmetsch, the doyenne of English viol players, to pay a visit to her summer viol school in Great Offley, Hitchin, Hertfordshire, and to play a solo recital on August 15. It was there that a long friendship began with Layton Ring, who provided me with a most sensitive harpsichord accompaniment for the recital. Linguist, poet, translator of fables of La Fontaine, native New Zealander -- he was a delightful companion during our collaborations in England. He and his wife, Christine, a fine baroque flutist, lived in Newcastle-upon-Tyne, where Layton was harpsichordist of the Northern Sinfonia Ensemble.

Layton Ring with his harpsichord van

While visiting the Dolmetsch family, I was attracted to and able to order a Barack Norman viola da gamba that was available for sale. Because it needed some restoration work, I settled on a price and left it there to be fixed. By the time I returned the next year to claim it and pay for it, the exchange rate had moved very much in my favor, so the delay was well worth the wait.

In 1967 I played in an eclectic series of three concerts in Rutherford College of the University of Northumbria at Newcastle. A large poster with stars and red and white stripes, advertising the concerts, hinted at their American origin. The first one featured Duke Ellington, the third was a blues and folk concert, and mine was billed as the Northern Sinfonia Ensemble with soloist Johnny Hsu!

It was at my recital in Edinburgh, Scotland, in 1967 that I met the Bach scholar, organist, and harpsichordist Peter Williams, who was then on the music faculty of Edinburgh University. He was also the director of the famous Russell Collection of Keyboard Instruments housed in the University's St Cecilia's Hall Museum of Instruments. I was delighted to be invited to play with him in subsequent years in beautiful St. Cecilia's Hall. We found we had so much in common in our musical taste, judgment, and interests that we soon became fast friends.

Rehearsing at our home in Ithaca, with Peter Williams

74

Traveling with a Large Instrument

Carrying the gamba on an airplane was much easier in the 1960's and 1970's than it is now. Security was lax and musical instruments were generally welcome, for half fare. With the appearance in commercial service of the Boeing 747 in 1970, I could request a block of four seats between the two aisles for Martha, the gamba, and me, and because the planes were seldom fully booked, the extra seat was usually available.

One year in London, the unusual shape of the gamba case caught the eye of a BOAC Passenger Officer, Henry Adler, who thereafter was on hand to help when travel arrangements hit a snag, once going so far as putting me up in his home when a flight was cancelled. (Coincidentally, it turned out that he had a cousin who lived near Ithaca, in Binghamton, New York!)

On one short flight between Frankfurt and Berlin, there was inexplicably no seat for the gamba, but the enterprising steward solved the problem by locking the instrument in one of the lavatories, changing the little sign to "*Besetzt*." ("Occupied") How times have changed! On a domestic flight in more recent years, the coach seat I had purchased turned out not to conform to the latest of the airline's rules, which specified that an instrument had to be "seated" just behind the bulkhead. The agent at the counter maintained that the bulkhead in this particular aircraft was in first class. So I had to pay for the instrument to be in first class, while I remained in coach.

The Summer Viol Program

My travels around Europe reinforced my awareness that there was no summer program devoted solely to the viola da gamba, and certainly none with an emphasis on French solo playing. In July of 1966, a summer school for viol players was appended to the International Recorder School held at Skidmore College. (I was one of four gambists who performed and taught there.) But opportunities to focus on the gamba alone were rare.

So in 1970, I started the Cornell Summer Viol Program with the intention of promulgating French Baroque solo viol music and teaching the technique necessary to perform it stylistically. Held on the Cornell campus that year from July 1 to 15, the program had 26 participants, although some were not there the entire time. There were amateurs, professional players and faculty from other institutions who ranged in age from a college freshman to a retired couple. When I announced the program I had no idea how many people might be interested in attending but, as it turned out, the response was so enthusiastic that I asked Barbara Mueser and Gian Lyman to help me teach. There were also two student assistants -- Richard Taruskin and Bonney McDowell, both graduate students at Columbia University at the time. The staff harpsichordist was Alexander Silbiger.

The daily schedule consisted of two 90-minute classes in the morning, one in consort playing and the other in solo performance. The rest of the day was for practice and rehearsals. The faculty gave one formal public concert and there were two informal student concerts. The faculty concert consisted of half a program of consort music and half of music by Marais and Forqueray.

After a hiatus of two summers, the program resumed in 1973, this time smaller, and designed primarily for qualified players who were eager to recapture the lost solo tradition of French viol playing of the 17th and 18th centuries. I continued to hold this program for 24 years; the last one was in the summer of 1997, with a week of Forqueray. Thereafter my arthritic fingers forced me to bring it to an end.

It was through participants' repeated attendance at this annual summer program that many of my close and lasting friendships were formed. Numerous former participants are now counted among this country's leading viola da gamba players. It was mainly due to their enthusiastic efforts, along with the support of the Viola da Gamba Society of America and The Hull Memorial Publication Fund of Cornell University, that a DVD was made of a class from the 1992 Cornell Summer Viol Program. This video is now distributed by the Viola da Gamba Society of America.

A NEW VIDEO

The Viola da Gamba Society of America

presents

JOHN HSU

In a Course
on
French Baroque
Viol Playing

Cornell Summer
Viol Program

Indigo Productions
New York

This video can be purchased from
The Viola da Gamba Society of America, 1308 Jackson Avenue, Charleston, IL 61920-2242
Price: $35.00 plus $5.00 postage and handling

A Handbook of French Baroque Viol Technique by John Hsu can be purchased from the publisher, Broude Brothers Limited,
141 White Oaks Road, Williamstown, MA 02167.
Tel.: 1-800-225-3197

Viol consort in 1970: Gian Lyman, Bonney McDowell, John Hsu, Barbara Mueser, Richard Taruskin

Viol consort in 1995: John Hsu, Roz Morley, Roland Hutchinson, Brent Wissick, Martha Bishop, Selina Carter

The Cremonese Viola da Gamba

Forqueray's son mentioned that his father had two viols that he used for many years, one for solo work, the other for accompaniment. It had been

my hope to find two historic viols whose tonal color would match when played together. But when William Monical informed me of the availability of a seven-string instrument made in Cremona in 1697, attributed to Francesco Ruggieri, I decided to go ahead and acquire the smaller, solo model. This viol, in design and style very French, is the only instrument of such small size in existence -- the string length is suited for ease of left hand movement demanded by the virtuoso literature. It appeared in the "Shapes of the Baroque" exhibition at Lincoln Center in 1989.

After I had played this viol, I realized that it would be well-nigh impossible to find a continuo viol to match its sweet, eloquent sound, so I abandoned my earlier hope. But my time with the instrument did allow me to experience firsthand the satisfaction of playing a viol that was constructed with the full range of French expressive effects in mind.

A Handbook of French Baroque Viol Technique

Among the viol treatises that I acquired in Paris, the most significant and pertinent one was the treatise in manuscript by Etienne Loulié entitled *Méthode pour apprendre à jouer la viole,* (ca. 1690). With much assistance from my helpful colleagues/friends in the Cornell Romance Literature Department, Professor Alain Seznec and the late Professor Edward Morris, in deciphering the idiosyncratic script of this 17th century author, I distilled the information conveyed in the manuscript, and adapted and applied its basic ideas in my own playing and teaching. Convinced of the efficacy of Loulié's approach, I used his treatise and those of his contemporaries, as well as musical sources, to write the Handbook, which was published by Broude Brothers Limited in 1981.

The Handbook was intended for players who had already mastered the basics of playing the viol and who wished to learn more about historically valid techniques for performing music composed in late 17th and early 18th century France. After discussing the techniques as recovered from contemporary sources, both theoretical and musical, I presented exercises to facilitate mastery of those techniques, illustrated by examples from Marais's and Forqueray's works.

The Marais Edition

In 1971, unbeknownst to me, the late Irving Broude of Broude Brothers Limited had the idea of publishing a modern edition of the complete instrumental works of Marin Marais. On the advice of François Lesure, I was offered the editorship. Little did I know that thirty years would pass before the edition was completed! Throughout those years, I had the benefit of the guiding hand of Dr. Ronald Broude (Irving's son), who, with his expert staff, provided all necessary support and invaluable advice in every aspect of the editorial and publication process.

Marin Marais is remembered and celebrated for his seven volumes of printed instrumental works. The most significant of these are the five volumes of *Pièces de violes*, published between 1686 and 1725, containing 598 pieces for viol and continuo. In addition, there is a volume of *Pièces en trio*, containing 67 pieces for two treble instruments and continuo, and *La Gamme et autres morceaux de simphonie* for violin, viol, and harpsichord.

The first editorial decision I made was to have all the works published in full scores, unlike the original editions, which were in part-books -- one for the solo gamba and one for the continuo player(s). I copied out every piece by hand, scoring it as I went, so as to provide the engraver with manuscripts on which to base his work. Marais's pieces were meticulously notated and richly decorated and we had to find an engraver who could have new punches made for all the *agréments* signs that are peculiar to French viol pieces. In the introductory matter of each volume I described the editorial policies and included an explanation of the signs indicating bowing, fingering, and ornaments.

The most difficult and time-consuming part of the edition was collating the different sources of each of the books. I wanted the edition to reflect, as far as possible, the composer's last revisions so I attempted to reconstruct a chronology based on addresses, contemporary catalogs, and the musical variants themselves. The first book had eleven early editions to be collated. The second book had the most revisions, containing over 1,000 variants[2].

While working on the edition, I recorded selected works from each of the first five books for The Musical Heritage Society. My good fortune in having excellent and congenial musical collaborators continued in these five recordings. The harpsichordist Louis Bagger played in all of them, and the continuo viol part was played by the incomparable Judith Davidoff. These recordings were made possible by a grant by The Hull Memorial Publication Fund of Cornell University.

By 1995, I became eager to speed up the progress of the remaining four volumes of the Marais edition, in order to assure its completion before my retirement. So it seemed like the right moment to devote more time and effort to work on completing this major project by giving up teaching and playing the cello, the main and constant part of my duty at Cornell for forty years. Thus I went on a half-time appointment at Cornell beginning in 1996 and taught a lighter load – conducting the Chamber Orchestra and coaching string quartets.

At this moment, computer technology entered the scene to replace the traditional engraving process used for the first three volumes, and instantaneous e-mail communication replaced the slower, round-trip airmail, thus giving the Marais project a much-needed boost. The result was the publication in quick succession of the last four volumes in five years: 1998, 2000, 2001, and 2002.

The significance of Marais' instrumental works extends beyond their inherent musical worth. These seven volumes, with the composer's meticulous and detailed notation, are the single most important musical source of information on performance practice of that period. I am extremely pleased that the resulting five volumes are not only owned by libraries but are widely used by performing musicians.

---

[2] "The First modern edition of the instrumental works of Marin Marais (1656-1728)," by John Hsu. *Fontes Artis Musicae*, vol. 52/1, January-March 2005.

The viol part

The continuo part

Both parts copied by me into a score

The Cornell University Trio/The Amadé Trio

In 1956, with the appointment of Sheldon Kurland as the new violin instructor, the enthusiastic agreement of my pianist colleague Ivan Waldbauer, and the blessing of Department Chairman Donald Grout, I founded the Cornell University Trio. This was a much-welcomed development, as it came at a time when few concerts were presented by the department. Ivan Waldbauer left Cornell for Brown University the following year and was succeeded by Daniel Eller. The Trio performed not only on campus and at neighboring colleges, we also recorded each week during the academic year a 30-minute trio program for broadcast on the Cornell FM radio station WHCU on Sunday morning.

The Trio gained wider recognition with its tour in Massachusetts during 1959-60, which included performances in Jordan Hall at the New England Conservatory of Music, the Isabella Stewart Gardner Museum in Boston, and the Phillips Academy in Andover. In 1960-61 the Trio was chosen by the Music Division of the Library of Congress for participation in its program of exchange among leading university resident ensembles, leading to concerts at the University of Illinois in Urbana, the University of Michigan in Ann Arbor, and the University at Buffalo. Despite changes in personnel, the Trio continued to be active through the 1960's, performing 68 times between 1956 and 1974.

The fervor of the authentic instrument movement (as it was called then) spread quickly in the 1970's, leading to many new ensembles and musical organizations that supported and propagated concerts of early music on period instruments (as they are called now). I was fortunate to be able to have my anonymous French cello restored to its original proportions by Frank Hubbard, the harpsichord maker. With drawings and measurements of an original instrument in hand, he turned this 18th century instrument back into a close approximation of what it had been when it was made. With the proper bow and a reëducated bow arm, I was able to produce a lighter, clearer, more resonant sound.

Thus in 1976 the Cornell University Trio was transformed into the Amadé Trio. It was certainly in the vanguard of the period instrument movement, and for several years enjoyed the enviable position as the premier fortepiano (early piano) trio in this country, with fortepianist Malcolm Bilson, violinist Sonya Monosoff, and myself as cellist. In addition to regular concerts, we performed so often in conjunction with scholarly symposiums and other musicological gatherings that some musicians jokingly called us the resident trio of the American Musicological Society. We specialized in works of Haydn, Mozart, and Beethoven on period instruments. Our recording of three Haydn Trios was issued by Titanic Records.

The Amadé Trio: John Hsu, Malcolm Bilson, Sonya Monosoff

From the 15th to the 20th Centuries

Meanwhile there had been, for a period of time, a slow and gradual increase of incoming students at Cornell who were proficient in playing early wind instruments (krummhorns, recorders, and shawms). They, together with a viol consort and singers, made a versatile and lively group. The Music Department began in 1977 to offer the Collegium Musicum as a course in the study and performance of Renaissance and Baroque music. Thus, the original purpose for acquiring the chest of viols in 1960 was finally realized.

In order to direct this new ensemble, I relinquished teaching music theory, after doing it for 22 years. The Collegium gradually attracted graduate students who were capable players of early instruments and who wished to gain some experience in directing such a group as part of their professional training. By the mid 1980s, the reins of the Collegium Musicum were handed over to graduate students.

At the same time, there began a sudden influx of better and better string players among the incoming undergraduates, so many that the Cornell Symphony Orchestra alone could not accommodate all of them. Thus in 1986 I formed the Cornell Chamber Orchestra and became its director. This development led to a shift in my musical focus from the 16th and 17th centuries to the 18th through the 20th centuries. Henceforth, due to professional circumstances and the gradual onset of arthritis in my hands, my career began to veer towards conducting.

Then in November of 1999, my colleague Edward Murray, conductor of the Cornell Symphony Orchestra, was struck down by pancreatic cancer, from which he did not recover. I was called upon to conduct the orchestra for the rest of the academic year. Since that year with the orchestra proved successful, I was offered the opportunity to continue as its director. In those last five years before my retirement, the Cornell Symphony Orchestra and I shared the joy of performing quite a list of great orchestral works. Among them were all nine symphonies of Beethoven, symphonies by Haydn, Mozart, Schubert, Mendelssohn,

Schumann, Brahms, Dvorak, Franck, and other major works by Fauré, Debussy, Hindemith, Prokofiev, and Stravinsky.

At one of the last rehearsals of the orchestra, I looked down at the violin sections and was struck by how many of the students were Asian, mostly Chinese. I could not resist telling them that, when I arrived at Cornell in 1955 and for many years after, there were no, or very few, Asian students in music. How times had changed!

In retrospect, I realized that performing music over these twenty-eight years, moving from the 15th to the 20th century, had given me a unique perspective on the repertoire. I was able to recognize and appreciate the gradual evolution of musical style as a natural outgrowth of what had gone before.

Aston Magna

In 1973, Albert Fuller, the distinguished American harpsichordist then teaching at the Juilliard School of Music in New York, founded the Aston Magna Foundation for Music and began the Aston Magna Festival in Great Barrington, Massachusetts. This new music festival took place at the Aston Magna Estate during the month of June. It was the first summer festival in this country devoted not only to the presentation of concerts on period instruments, but also with the aim of doing so with a humanistic, inter-disciplinary approach. I was invited to be a member of its artist-faculty in 1974.

By then, a dozen or more fine young musicians were attending as associates, performing both as members of the orchestra and in chamber music. In jest they called themselves the B team. All of them and their students are now part of the A team of early music activities today. I believe that a majority of the leading players of period instruments in this country today can trace their musical lineage somehow to Aston Magna. Albert Fuller deserves much credit for raising the performance standard of period instruments during his years as Artistic Director. He was an inspiration to all who came into musical contact with him.

After Albert's retirement in 1983, the virtuoso recorder player Bernard Krainis was appointed interim director in 1984, and I became the Director of Aston Magna from 1985 to 1990. In that capacity I was ably and loyally supported by soprano Sally Sanford as Assistant Director. She was at once a first-rate musician and an excellent administrator.

This highly acclaimed Festival had by then become this country's longest-running annual summer festival devoted to concerts of 17th and 18th century music on period instruments. During this time we extended our concert activities to Bard College at Annandale-on-Hudson, New York, and Rutgers University in New Brunswick, New Jersey.

We also expanded Aston Magna's offerings by introducing the Aston Magna Performance Practice Institute in 1986 and 1990. Designed for performers of professional caliber, the Institute offered an unprecedented, intensive, performance-oriented program on specific topics to complement the broad humanistic view of music and its surrounding culture provided by the Aston Magna Academy in 1985, 1987, and 1989. These were the last three of the series of eight Aston Magna Academies (supported by the National Endowment for the Humanities), the brainchild of its inspiring and experienced director, Raymond Erickson. They contributed to the enrichment of the Aston Magna experience in ways that I have not encountered anywhere else.

Interviewed by Allan Kozinn for his article about Aston Magna in the *New York Times* on July 22, 1988 ("For Authenticity, More than Early Instruments"), I had a chance to elaborate on my ideas about period instrument performance: "People jump to the conclusion that using early instruments automatically means that a performance will be authentic, but that's too simpleminded. The instrument doesn't make music for you. The player has to understand what the notation he is looking at is trying to tell him, because although most notation looks the same, composers working in different countries, and at different times, used it to indicate different things. So, historically informed performance is part of it. But even that's not enough. You have to come up with a historically informed performance that is also emotionally involved. Otherwise, it's going to be pretty dry."

Before becoming Aston Magna Director Emeritus in 1990, I conducted a small orchestra of musicians in performances of music by Corelli, Caldara, Handel, and Haydn, and the concert was issued as a CD by Titanic Records: *Live from Aston Magna Festival, 1990*. This group of musicians was the genesis, in principle if not totally in fact, of the Apollo Ensemble that I founded at the end of 1990.

The Haydn Baryton Trio

Aston Magna during the late 1970s was the setting that enabled me to revive the baryton trios (for baryton, viola, and cello) by Joseph Haydn. It was there that baroque violist David Miller and baroque cellist Fortunato (Freddie) Arico offered their enthusiastic and encouraging support to form The Haydn Baryton Trio in 1980.

The baryton is simply an instrument that is made up of a viola da gamba and a small harp. The neck of the viola da gamba is broadened so that the plucked strings can run behind it. These metal strings are strung either on a low bridge or on individual studs on the belly of the instrument. They are exposed within the open, boxlike back of the neck so that the left thumb can pluck them. Thus the playing technique of the baryton demands that the left hand function in two ways: fingering the bowed strings on the fingerboard and plucking the harp strings behind the neck. The baryton trio is the genre in which Haydn composed the largest number of works. He did so because his patron for many years, Prince Nicholas Esterhazy, was an ardent player of this instrument and demanded a constant supply of new works for his enjoyment and edification, playing trios with the court cellist and Haydn on the viola. All the baryton trios were composed between 1762 and 1775. Thereafter, the Prince's musical interest turned to the opera.

The baryton

David, Freddie, and I were eager to call attention to the baryton trios in time for the celebration of the 250th anniversary of the composer's birth in 1982. Until I was able to procure an instrument, we played early trios that did not call for plucked strings, but I was truly eager have a real baryton. My old friend Judy Davidoff alerted me to the fact that George Cassis, an experienced sound-reduction engineer in Baltimore, had already built several unusual instruments – a hurdy-gurdy, a baroque violin, and her own baryton. I approached him with the idea of commissioning a baryton for myself, explaining that I had the intention of doing a serious study of the magnificent trio repertoire, as yet seldom heard.

After a three-year wait, I got a call from Cassis letting me know that the baryton was finished. He said he had received very helpful advice about the construction from the authorities at the Collection of Historic Musical Instruments (*Sammlung alter Musikinstrumente*) in Vienna. I had stressed the Austro-Hungarian nature of the baryton to him, suggesting he give the varnish a reddish (paprika-like) hue. Still I was surprised when I picked it up to see how very red it was. Henceforth it was dubbed "Heinz."

The Haydn Baryton Trio quickly gained recognition with our two LPs of baryton trios by Haydn for The Musical Heritage Society in 1981 and 1982. They were the first recordings of Haydn baryton trios played on period instruments. (Although a couple of European recordings of Haydn baryton trios were already available, they were played with modern viola and cello, and hence were not totally satisfactory in terms of tonal color and balance.) These two recordings were re-issued as compact discs by Gaudeamus in London in 1986 and 1988. The second recording was chosen winner in the "Early Instrumental" category of The [English] Music Retailers Association's Annual Awards for Excellence in 1989.

The Haydn Baryton Trio was much in demand during 1982, the 250th anniversary of Haydn's birth, and, as engagements multiplied, I began to sense a need for a replacement baryton in case anything should happen to the first one. So I asked George Cassis to build a duplicate. This second baryton turned out to be sturdy and reliable, and seemed to possess a

more eloquent and easy nature than the first. It became my preferred
concert instrument.

John Hsu, David Miller, Fortunato Arico

In a program at the Smithsonian Institution in March of 1982, the Haydn Baryton Trio was joined by other instrumentalists for performances of Haydn's Baryton Quintet No. 2 in D Major and his Baryton Octet No. 4 in G Major. This was the only time we performed these works.

Our trio's revival of the baryton trios of Haydn was received with great enthusiasm everywhere. The following brief quote, from Daniel Webster's review of our concert in the *Philadelphia Inquirer* in 1982, represented a typical response of our audience:

What a view of Haydn's ebullient gifts this concert provided! John Hsu, playing a baryton made by George Cassis of Baltimore, showed a polished technique that had the appeal of musicality and the charm of magic. When the strings are plucked from behind the broad neck of the instrument, it appears that the instrument is singing by itself... The concert was far from merely novel. Hsu's colleagues used instruments strung with gut and played with slight vibrato to create a strongly balanced ensemble. Both instruments had been restored to 18th century standards of lighter sound. The baryton's sympathetic strings resound at cadences, so the music was shaped to let that sound float up clearly... This was not an academic restoration but a musical discovery in which the players caught the vitality of the writing.

Tragedy struck with the death of Fortunato Arico in 1984, soon after our performance in the Mostly Mozart Festival at Avery Fisher Hall in Lincoln Center in New York on August 2, 1984. An ideal collaborator, a wonderful musician, a loyal friend, Freddie's participation in the rebirth of the Haydn Baryton Trio was far too short.

Loretta O'Sullivan succeeded him the following year.

John Hsu, Loretta O'Sullivan, David Miller

In November of 1989, The Haydn Baryton Trio traveled to England to perform at Wigmore Hall in London and in the Sheldonian Theatre at Oxford University. Two memories stand out. While in London, Martha went out to get a newspaper and brought back the news that the Berlin Wall had come down the night before! And in Oxford, I kept remembering that Haydn himself had received an Honorary Doctorate in the Sheldonian Theatre in 1791. At the time he was embarking on his highly successful sojourns in England (where his works were prized), but he surely would have found it incredible that his baryton trios, written as house music for the Prince, would be performed in the same space 198 years later.

In 1994, thanks to the dedicated efforts of our wonderful concert manager and dear friend Joyce Rohr of Rohr Artists Management, The Haydn Baryton Trio received an invitation to perform at the Esterhazy Palace in Eisenstadt, Austria. Less than 40 miles from Vienna, this is the palace where Haydn spent many years in the employ of Prince Nikolaus Esterhazy. We took the opportunity to do a little Haydn pilgrimage. We visited his birthplace in Rohrau, about 30 miles from Vienna; we saw the other palace that Nikolaus built for himself, Esterháza, now in Hungary at Fertöd; we saw the house he had lived in when he first went to Vienna and the house in Vienna where he died; most of all we enjoyed touring his home in Eisenstadt and retracing his steps up the street to the palace where he worked.

Playing in the space for which the music was written was indeed a thrilling and broadening experience. The acoustics were so perfect for the music that we came to the realization that the composer wrote the music not just for the designated instruments but also for that particular venue.

In 1996 we made a CD of six Haydn trios for Dorian Recordings. This recording included the only extended example of simultaneous bowing and plucking by the solo baryton player in the entire corpus of the baryton trios by Haydn: the trio section of the *Menuet* in Trio 107 in D Major.

The Haydn Baryton Trio continued to perform until my arthritis compelled us to stop in the summer of 1997, after our performance at the Bard (College) Music Festival.

The Five-String Cello

It is widely believed that J. S. Bach's sixth suite for unaccompanied cello (Suite No. 6 in D major, BWV 1012) was composed specifically for a five-string violoncello piccolo -- a slightly smaller cello that has a fifth upper string tuned to E. When, after his death, Freddie Arico's five-string cello came on the market, I bought it, mainly to explore the full effectiveness of playing the sixth suite on it.

The primary importance of a fifth string – a high first string pitched at E – is in the sonority of an open E and the more relaxed sound of high notes. Bach capitalized on this expanded range and greater resonance throughout the sixth suite. He wrote the Prelude in a kind of ritornello form, alternating the musical material of the tutti and solo sections. The main figure for the tutti section is identified by the presence of the pedal point. The extra string makes available four pedal-points, G, D, A, and E providing an extension of the excitement of the harmonic sequences that give this movement its rhythmic drive.

In 1987 I took the five-string cello on tour, combining a short lecture with a performance of the sixth suite. While in Chapel Hill, our friend David Hughes made a video of me playing the suite in his living room. We later turned this VHS tape into a CD, and will eventually put it on YouTube.

When I decided to sell the cello, I remembered someone who had expressed interest in it at the time of Freddie's death, so I called her and arranged a very unusual transfer. She lived in New Jersey; Martha and I were driving to New York to fly to Aruba for a vacation in January, so we agreed to meet at the side of the highway, close to where Interstate 80 crosses Interstate 287. This was hardly an ideal place to transact a sale, with heavy traffic flying by, but we managed. She handed me a check, I gave her the cello, and we both drove off.

The Apollo Ensemble

After our baryton trio concerts at Esterhazy Palace, my fascination with Haydn's life and my love for his music continued to grow unabated. From the moment I started to play the baryton trios, I was struck by the overall musical contrast that one finds between these trios and his early symphonies from the same period. The trios on the whole contain more intimate, somber and melancholic music, and the symphonies more extroverted, brilliant, and cheerful music. It is as though the composer was taking advantage of the differences between the tonal colors of the two ensembles, trio and orchestra, to express the full range of his musical feeling and reveal different aspects of his personality.

Having had the experience of conducting some of Haydn's early, baryton-trio-period symphonies at Aston Magna, I was eager to capture a fuller musical portrait of the composer with a small ensemble of period instruments, so I founded the Apollo Ensemble in December of 1990. In hopes of recapturing the tonal qualities and balance of the orchestra for which Haydn composed these symphonies, the Apollo Ensemble duplicated both the size (fourteen players) and the instrumentation of the orchestra at Esterhazy Palace.

The Apollo Ensemble took off like a jet. We played our initial two concerts during the summer of 1991 at Cornell, and made our New York City debut at Merkin Concert Hall in New York City that fall. With a tape recording of that concert as a sample, we got a contract with Dorian Recordings for our first CD of early Haydn symphonies. Comprising Nos. 35 in B-flat Major, 23 in G Major, and 42 in D Major, it was entitled "Symphonies for the Esterhazy Court," and was nominated for the 1996 Cannes Classical Awards in the category of Orchestral Music 17/18th Century.

The second CD (Symphonies Nos. 12 in E Major, 64 in A Major, and 44 in E Minor), also from Dorian Recordings, was made in 1995. In a review in *Alte Musik Aktuell*, Regensburg, Germany, (2/96) Robert Strobl said, "Und der Haydn kommt so locker – wie ein Salzburger Nockerl, höast." Although the review appeared to be positive, I wondered what the analogy to *Salzburger Nockerl* implied. When Martha and I soon thereafter had the opportunity to try this dessert, we were delighted to find ourselves served a delicious, fluffy, egg white concoction.

For the third CD, (Symphonies Nos. 28 in A Major, 18 in G Major, and 52 in C Minor), recorded in Jordan Hall at the New England Conservatory of Music in 1998 and issued by Centaur Records, I was pleased to have permission to use on the cover the painting of Haydn done in 1806 by Isidor Neugass. It portrays Haydn with a statue of Apollo in a niche and a portrait of J.S. Bach, seen faintly behind.

In 1997, The Apollo Ensemble was awarded a grant from The Fund for U.S. Artists at International Festivals and Exhibition, a public/private partnership of the National Endowment for the Arts, the United States Information Agency, the Rockefeller Foundation, and the Pew Charitable Trusts, to perform concerts of symphonies of Joseph Haydn at two of the most renown early music festivals in Europe: *Tage Alter Musik* in Regenburg, Germany, and *Joseph Haydn – Festspiele* in Eisenstadt, Austria.

It was on this tour that I first fully appreciated the proximity of European countries and major cities. For the five days between our Regensburg concert on May 17 and our Eisenstadt concert on May 23, our friend and manager Joyce Rohr was able to schedule four more concerts to make up a tour. All of them took place at historical places that were worth visiting, with or without music.

In Regensburg, a city that had suffered little damage from Allied bombing, the Apollo Ensemble performed in the *Minoritenkirche,* a concert hall originally built as a church in 1226. We arrived in Regensburg the day before the concert, so we had time to do some sightseeing and to eat at the oldest continuously operating sausage house in town, birthplace of the bratwurst.

The Cistercian Maulbronn Monastery, northwest of Stuttgart, is considered the most complete and best-preserved medieval monastic complex north of the Alps, and is a UNESCO World Heritage site. On May 18, we opened the monastery's concert series with a gala concert celebrating the 850th anniversary of the monastery's founding. In attendance on this festive occasion were prominent political leaders and important church representatives.

We spent the next day traveling to the Czech Republic in our large, elegant bus, which was hired for the entire tour. It is a bus the likes of which I have not yet seen in this country. One of its comfortable features was the movability of the aisle seats towards the center so as to get more elbow room when traveling long distance.

Our three concerts in the Czech Republic were in contrasting historical buildings on three consecutive nights, May 20-22, the first one in the castle in Nelahozeves (birthplace of Dvořák), the second in the Moravian Gallery in Brno, and the last in the St. Barbara Church in Adamov. The acoustics were wonderful in all the places.

Since we were housed in a resort hotel in Blansko, near the Moravian Karst, we found time to visit the amazing Punkva Caves in spite of our tight concert schedule. There for the first time I saw stalagmites and stalactites close-up for the first time. Another unexpected event was the Blansko Mayor's official welcome of the Apollo Ensemble, at which I was presented with a key to the city.

The reception after the third concert, hosted by the Adamov Chorus, was one of the happiest and most memorable events of the tour, even though none of us spoke Czech and only a few of our hosts spoke English. So it was a mostly non-verbal friendly night of dancing, drinking, singing and feasting.

Finally, on to Esterhazy Palace in Eisenstadt, Austria, to discover as closely as possible what Haydn's early symphonies sounded like when they were first heard there over two hundred years ago. The musicians were housed in *Zum Eder*, the oldest inn in town, which opened in 1592.

As the following short excerpt from the fall 1998 issue of the *New England Conservatory Notes* so aptly reported:

"*In 1991 he [Hsu] continued this exploration by founding the Apollo Ensemble for the sole purpose of playing Haydn's pre-1775 symphonies with a close replica of his own orchestra. Without planning it, Hsu was suddenly a leading specialist and ready to take this music back to its place of birth. Hsu's ensemble hit Europe with a tour that ended at the Esterhazy Palace where the works were first played. The reaction to this coals-to-Newcastle diplomatic mission was sensational. The key word in German reviews was "Spannung" ("excitement"). Most telling of all was critics' discernment of the "organic" element in this European debut by Americans playing key works of European heritage. Hsu's reverse import had succeeded in closing a cultural circle.*"

The Apollo Ensemble in Europe

The Creation

I chose to mark my official retirement from Cornell on March 12, 2005, by conducting a performance of *The Creation* by Joseph Haydn with a professional festival orchestra and the incomparable Cornell University Chorus and Glee Club, Scott Tucker, Director. I had loved this work for many years and was eager to conduct it using the latest edition, published in 1995 by Oxford University Press and edited by A. Peter Brown. This edition was based on original orchestra and vocal parts used for the first performances in Vienna, and included contemporary accounts of those performances. It revealed a far more descriptive and cohesive work than I had heard in previous performances or imagined in reading other editions of the score.

When I ordered the score from Oxford I was surprised to see that the format was smaller than the usual conductor's score. Fearing that I would not be able to see the music well enough when conducting, I immediately acquired reading glasses calibrated for the distance from my eyes to the stand. These reassured me that all would be well... until I started to worry that I might misplace these glasses. I duly ordered another pair, to have as a spare.

The night of the performance, with a full house and palpable excitement on the part of the orchestra, chorus and audience, I went to the podium, acknowledged the applause, turned around to face the performers, and gave the downbeat for beginning the piece. Only then did I realize that I did not have either pair of glasses on! Of course I had to continue conducting and fortunately knew the score well enough to get through without faltering. This success contributed to my forgetting my glasses again for the second half of the concert!

The long applause and my repeated curtain calls at the end of *The Creation* I recognized as the Cornell/Ithaca audience's thanks for my fifty years of concerts. Never did I imagine, when I arrived at Cornell in 1955, that I would participate in such a variety of musical performances and end my professional life as a conductor!

104

Leaving Ithaca

Martha and I had fully expected to live out our lives in Ithaca, New York, but fate decided otherwise. When we retired from Cornell in 2005 (Martha after 38 years in various challenging and satisfying positions in the library system and I after 50 years of teaching), I found myself no longer able to bear the long, hard winters of Ithaca. Our families were scattered across the country but we had friends from various stages of our lives living in the Chapel Hill and Durham, North Carolina, area, so we began spending our winters in the Triangle and relocated there permanently in September 2010. We moved to Carol Woods, a continuing care retirement community, in September 2012.

We left Ithaca with heavy hearts. In important ways, it will always be "home" to both of us. The years there had been richly blessed with abundant opportunities for new musical explorations, thrilling performances, professional satisfaction, and, best of all, a multitude of valued friendships.

402 Hanshaw Road, Ithaca, NY 14850

Atlanta Baroque Orchestra

A smooth transition into post-retirement conducting activities occurred when I was invited to guest conduct the Atlanta Baroque Orchestra in Atlanta, Georgia, in January of 2004, which led to my accepting the position of Artistic Director and Conductor of the orchestra. From 2005 to 2009, I thoroughly enjoyed performing a wide range of Baroque and Classical orchestral music with this top-notch professional period-instrument group.

One Friday in 2008, our baroque horn player, Russell Williamson, picked me up at the hotel for an afternoon rehearsal. Russell was also the personnel manager of the Atlanta Symphony Orchestra. On this day, soon after we left for Buckhead, Russell started to tell me with great enthusiasm about the orchestra's new Assistant Conductor, a Chinese woman by the name of Mei-Ann Chen. In the midst of his accolade for this fine musician, while we were in the heavy traffic of Peachtree Road, the traffic light suddenly changed to red, and Russell turned to me with disbelief and said: "there she is," pointing to the car to our left. He and Mei-Ann rolled down their car windows, and Russell introduced us to each other. When the traffic light changed to green, we continued on our way in total disbelief that such a chance encounter could really have occurred with such exact timing.

I have to confess that I was so dazed by such a coincidence that I had trouble concentrating at the rehearsal that followed. But I managed, and we had a productive rehearsal. About three hours later we were back on Peachtree Road for the return trip to the hotel, when once again we had to stop at a red traffic light. Lo and behold! On our left was Mei-Ann Chen again! We were flabbergasted and speechless. What are the odds of such a chance meeting happening twice in a matter of hours in the same day?

Regrettably, because of conflicts between our rehearsal and concert schedules, we were unable to attend each other's concerts. Therefore, I was touched by her amiable presence at my rehearsal the next day. So thanks to her initiative we met for the third time in Atlanta!

Three Vivaldi Project Concerts and a Birthday

On October 9 and 11, 2009, I guest-conducted the Vivaldi Project Ensemble of Washington, DC, one of the finest ensembles of period stringed instruments today, in two performances -- in Bethesda, Maryland, and in Washington, D. C. I called the program "Threads of Inspiration." It consisted of a violin concerto by Vivaldi, three *Sinfonias* of C.P.E. Bach, and a Mozart piano concerto (Andrew Willis, fortepiano). It is hard to imagine that Bach would have created such difficult violin parts without Vivaldi's advanced violin vocabulary and idioms, as formulated in his violin concertos. In turn, these C.P.E. Bach *Sinfonias* must have inspired subsequent composers to write more imaginative orchestral violin parts. They, along with Vivaldi's concertos, constituted a forceful impetus that let to the emotional and dramatic music of Mozart and other composers of the Classical Period.

In 2010, again as guest conductor of the Vivaldi Project, I had the satisfying experience of conducting the complete six *Sinfonias* for strings, W. 182, by C.P.E. Bach. These demanding works had intrigued me for over thirty years, but I had never thought that I would have the chance to perform all of them. There were three performances -- in Winston Salem and Durham, North Carolina, and then in Bethesda, Maryland, on September 19. This last performance was recorded and released, unedited, by Centaur Records.

On September 6, 2013, I celebrated Martha's birthday and the 365th day since we moved into Carol Woods with a concert, in the Carol Woods Assembly Hall, of two Haydn symphonies (No. 23 and No. 47) played by musicians from the Chapel Hill/Triangle area on modern instruments. I was glad to demonstrate, once again, that much of the composer's expressive range and phrasing can be conveyed effectively on modern instruments. Players with the ability to alter their bow strokes vis-à-vis tension, speed, weight, and variety manage to achieve, to a great degree, important characteristics of period instruments. Above all, a performer with a lively imagination regarding the basic character of the music itself will be able somehow to use the bow arm to produce the appropriate effect.

Mozart concert at Carol Woods on September 6, 2013

Then in February 2014 I guest-conducted The Vivaldi Project in three performances on consecutive nights of works for strings by Caldara, Corelli, Handel, Vivaldi, W.F. Bach and C.P.E. Bach. These concerts, titled "C.P.E. Bach and his Dramatic Predecessors," took place at Carol Woods, in Hill Hall on the University of North Carolina campus, and at UNC Greensboro. As collaborators I had the good fortune to be working once again with the expert string players of this ensemble, led by my former students, violinist Elizabeth Field, and cellist Stephanie Vial. Both are specialists in historical performance practice who received their doctorates at Cornell University. They and others who have worked with me have developed a shorthand communication of their own. The mention of a two-bow gesture here, for instance, or a jetté there, is instantly understandable.

The Vivaldi Ensemble before the concert in Hill Hall, February 6, 2014

Thereafter my health has precluded the intense music-making that had been my joy. Despite my profound sense of loss, I am aware of my abundance of good fortune, both personal and professional, and am grateful for having had a life full of music.

Appendix 1
Additional Professional Highlights

1971: Honorary Doctor of Music Degree

A most gratifying event took place on May 23, 1971, when the President of the New England Conservatory, the composer Gunther Schuller, conferred upon me the Honorary Doctor of Music degree at the commencement exercises. Not only had this honor from my alma mater come as a surprise, but to receive it on the stage of Jordan Hall along with three celebrities whom I so admired was totally unexpected. They were Arthur Fiedler, the famous conductor of the Boston Pops Orchestra, Frederick Jagel, retired head of the voice department at NEC who hired me as one of his studio accompanists when I was an undergraduate, and Coretta Scott King, who was an alumna of NEC.

1974 & 1998: The Passions

In April of 1974, I played the viola da gamba solos in the St. Matthew Passion with the Chicago Symphony Orchestra, Sir Georg Solti conducting. As it turned out, my last public performance on the gamba was in the St. John Passion at Cornell in 1998.

1975: The Smithsonian Tour: "Music & Dance from the Age of Jefferson"

In anticipation of the Bicentennial, the Smithsonian Institution initiated a concert tour in the fall of 1975 to illustrate the musical taste and personal ability of Thomas Jefferson as a violinist. To this end, I was fortunate to have been invited to participate in a small group of musicians, expert on 18th century instruments and cognizant of the musical style of the time, to perform music from Jefferson's library. We were fitted in colonial costumes and sent on a tour across the country, culminating in a concert in San Francisco.

As a colonial musician

1981: Spring Term spent at the University of California, Davis, as Artist-in-Residence
1983: Spring Term spent at the University of California, Santa Cruz, as Regents' Lecturer

One of the pleasures of a visitor is the opportunity to perform music in different venues, with able collaborators, for new discerning audiences; both of these California appointments were satisfying and fruitful. Going to and from Davis, Martha and I drove across the country, experiencing for the first time its grandeur and beauty.

1986 – 1993: Concerts with the Theorbo

Sources from 17th and early 18th century France stress that the sound for which French viol players of the time strove was one which had an attack similar to the plucking of the lute or harpsichord. In Hubert le Blanc's description of Marais's playing, he says that Marais's bow strokes resembled the plucking of the lute and guitar. This intriguing description inspired me to want to explore the sonority resulting from combining two plucked instruments – one plucked with the bow and the other with fingers.

When Catherine Liddell arrived at Aston Magna with her theorbo, we had the opportunity to experiment with sound. Subsequently, Cathy and I succeeded in combining our palates of articulation to achieve a wider range of expressive consonants -- from the softer, finger-plucking of the theorbo to the bowed plucking of the viol. This seemed to enhance each instrument's versatility, especially in soft and expressive pieces.

With Cathy Liddell

2001: The *Chevalier*

Recognizing my accomplishments with the viola da gamba and its repertoire, my <u>Handbook of French Baroque Viol Technique</u>, the seven-volume Marais edition, and in general my promulgation of the French solo viol tradition, the French government conferred on me the *Chevalier de l'ordre des arts et des letters* (Knight of the Order of Arts and Letters) on February 27, 2001. Martha and I invited twenty of our friends and relatives to the ceremony, held at the French Embassy in New York City. I was presented with a slender green pin to be worn on a lapel and a large medal suspended from a green and white ribbon. Although enormously pleased by the honor, I have only worn the medal once – at a formal dinner party given by friends.

In my response to Pierre Buhler, Cultural Counselor of the Embassy of France, I expressed my wish that I could convey my gratitude to three great French spirits: to Louis XIV for making Lully his music master, to Lully for teaching Marais the art of musical composition, and to Marais for composing the largest and most beautiful corpus of some 600 pieces

for the gamba. I ended by saying, "For the enrichment that French music has given to my life and for the honor that I have received, I give France my boundless thanks."

The Chevalier

2003: An Outstanding Alumni Award

I received an Outstanding Alumni award from the New England
Conservatory in 2003 and presented a talk entitled "My Musical
Explorations." As I said then, "In retrospect, it seems that I undertook
new musical explorations with each new decade." The 60's – performing
solo French viol music. The 70's – the Amadé Trio and the Marais
edition. The 80's – The Haydn Baryton Trio and the 5-string cello. The
90's –The Apollo Ensemble, performing early Haydn symphonies. The
2000's – Conducting the Cornell Symphony Orchestra in all nine
Beethoven Symphonies. I went on, "These performances convinced me
once again that revisiting masterpieces with new information and insight
can be as exciting as exploring unknown or lesser-known musical
territories." I closed with an encouragement to pursue musical
explorations: "They have enriched my life, and I am sure they will enrich
yours."

Jordan Hall, NEC

Appendix 2
CD Discography

John Hsu, baryton

Baryton Trios by Joseph Haydn. Containing Trios No. 97 in D Major, No. 111 in G Major, No. 87 in A Minor, and No. 101 in C Major.
John Hsu, baryton; David Miller, viola; and Fortunato Arico, cello.
Gaudeamus. GAU 104 R
1986

Baryton Trios by Joseph Haydn. Vol 2. Containing Trios No. 71 in A Major, No. 113 in D Major, No. 96 in B Minor, and No. 126 in C Major.
John Hsu, baryton; David Miller, viola; and Fortunato Arico, cello.
Gaudeamus. GAU 109
Winner in the "Early Instrumental" Category of The Music Retailers Association's Annual Awards for Excellence, London, 1989.
1988

Haydn Divertimenti. Containing Trios No. 50 in D Major, No. 59 in G Major, No. 107 in D Major, No. 57 in A Major, No. 52 in D Major, and No. 67 in G Major.
John Hsu, baryton; David Miller, viola; and Loretta O'Sullivan, cello.
Dorian Recordings. DOR 90233
1996

John Hsu, Conductor

Live from Aston Magna Festival, 1990. John Hsu, Conductor.
Containing Concerto Grosso in G Minor, Op. 6, No. 8 by Arcangelo Corelli; Sinfonias No. 12 in A Minor, and No. 4 in B Minor by Antonio Caldara; Concerto Grosso in E Minor, Op. 6, No. 3 by George Frideric Handel; Symphony No. 47 in G Major by Franz Joseph Haydn.
Titanic Records. TI-192
1990

Symphonies for the Esterhazy Court. Containing symphonies by Franz Joseph Haydn: No. 35 in B-flat Major, No. 23 in G Major, and No. 42 in D Major.
Apollo Ensemble. John Hsu, Conductor
Dorian Recordings. DOR-90191
Nominated for the 1996 Cannes Classical Awards in the category of Orchestral Music 17/18th Century.
1994

The Hidden Haydn. Containing symphonies by Franz Joseph Haydn: No. 12 in E Major, No. 64 in A Major; and No. 44 in E Minor.
Apollo Ensemble. John Hsu, Conductor
Dorian Recordings. DOR-90226
1995

Joseph Haydn: Symphonies No. 28 in A Major, No. 18 in G Major, and No. 52 in C Minor.
Apollo Ensemble. John Hsu, Conductor
Centaur Records. CRC 2447
1998

Six Sinfonias for String Orchestra, W. 182. Containing Sinfonias III in C Major, V in B Minor, IV in A Major, VI in E Major, I in G Major, and II in B-flat Major.
The Vivaldi Project. John Hsu, Conductor
Recorded live and unedited.
Centaur Records. CRC 3176
September 19, 2010

Appendix 3
Selected Reviews

John Hsu... has won special distinction for his technical mastery, his authenticity of style, and for the unusual expressiveness of his playing.
> *The Evening Star* (Washington, D.C.) April 6, 1970

Playing his historic instrument with superb control, Hsu projected vital rhythm, smooth phrasing and singing tone.
> *The Plain Dealer*, Cleveland, May 22, 1971

Throughout these performances [Hsu] displays a profound understanding of Forqueray's musical language and is extremely adept at emphasizing all the elegance of expressiveness of the French style.
> *Hi-Fi News & Record Review* (London), July, 1973

In the six brief movements of the Baryton Trio No 97 in D "For the happiest birthday of Prince Esterhazy" [the] music-making was... intimate, beautifully blended, flexible and spontaneous.
> *The [London] Times*, November 17, 1989

Conductor John Hsu evinces many deft touches of accenting, particularly in the slow movements of these less well-known symphonies.... And the minuets...are a revelation of rhythmic vitality.
> *Soundscapes* (Windsor, Victoria, Australia) September–October 1994

The Apollo Ensemble under John Hsu inoculates [Haydn] Symphonies 12, 44, and 64 with a modern wit and grace, making them safe from romantic onslaughts for years to come.
> *Fanfare* (The Magazine for Serious Record Collections), March-April 1996

Hsu is a world-class virtuoso on the baryton...
> *American Record Guide*, May/June 1996

Hsu's straight-ahead conducting stabilized what had been shaky... Like a Michael Jordan, Hsu is the sort of performer who elevates the play of those around him. Whatever the secret, Hsu's got it.
> *The Atlanta Journal-Constitution*. September 28, 2004

Appendix 4
The Family

Nancy, John, Bella, Mother, Father, and Tom in Shanghai (1948?)

Parents' Fiftieth Wedding Anniversary in August 1979
Tom, Nancy, Father, Mother, John, and Bella in Toronto

My parents left China in 1960 and settled in Toronto, where my father was the pastor of the largest Chinese Presbyterian church in North America until he retired. He died in 1984 and my mother died in 2002.

Nancy and her husband, Paul, live in Glendale, California. Nancy had an active singing career in Hong Kong before they relocated to California. Their daughter, Violette, lives nearby and their son, Vincent, is in Hong Kong. They have one grandson.

Tom and his wife, Laura, live in Houston, Texas. Tom earned his Ph.D. in Civil Engineering at Cornell University and both their daughters attended Cornell University as graduate students. Mia lives in Austin, Texas, and Lynne lives in Albuquerque, New Mexico. Tom and Laura have four grandchildren.

Bella had a career as a demographer in Honolulu and has retired there. Her husband, Ted, has passed away. She has one son, Douglas, who lives in Sunnyvale, California, and one grandson.

Naturally there is much more that could be said about each family and indeed about each family member, but those stories are for them to tell.

Acknowledgements

Thanks go to:

Jan and Nat Justice for their early encouragement and helpful comments.

William Monical for information about the Cremonese viola da gamba.

Dot Boggess for suggesting the title.

Lynne Hsu Xavier for her scanned photographs of my grandparents and parents.

Gretchen Likins for her photographs of the Mozart concert in 2013.

David Hughes for his photograph of the Vivaldi Project Ensemble in 2014.

Robin Samuels for her copyediting of the memoir in its early stages.

Simon Glancey for permission to use the image of the Stratocruiser.

Erika Hamlett for helping with Word and the cover.

Personal Name Index

Wedding in Swatow, ca. 1935.
Ringboy in front.